DOWNSIZING
The Family Home

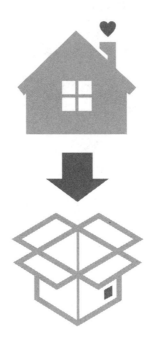

DOWNSIZING
The Family Home

WHAT TO SAVE, WHAT TO LET GO

Marni Jameson

FOREWORD BY MARK BRUNETZ

STERLING
New York

Real Possibilities

STERLING
New York

An Imprint of Sterling Publishing
1166 Avenue of the Americas
New York, NY 10036

ISBN 978-1-4549-1633-8

Distributed in Canada by Sterling Publishing
C/o Canadian Manda Group, 664 Annette Street
Toronto, Ontario, Canada M6S 2C8
Distributed in the United Kingdom by GMC Distribution Services
Castle Place, 166 High Street, Lewes, East Sussex, England BN7 1XU
Distributed in Australia by Capricorn Link (Australia) Pty. Ltd.
P.O. Box 704, Windsor, NSW 2756, Australia

For information about custom editions, special sales, and premium and corporate purchases,
please contact Sterling Special Sales at 800-805-5489 or
specialsales@sterlingpublishing.com.

Manufactured in Canada

11 10

www.sterlingpublishing.com

For my parents, Neal and Nancy Jameson,

who taught me the meaning of home.

Contents

Foreword

In *Downsizing the Family Home*, Marni Jameson takes us on a personal journey that promises to impart a new way of thinking when it comes to honoring what we as adult children treasure most: our parents and their legacy.

As cohost of *Clean House* on the Style Network for nearly a decade, I have had over 300 families from all over the United States open their homes and their hearts to me, contributing incredible insights into how to deal with a house full of stuff and a heart full of stories. The result was captured in my first book, *Take the U Out of Clutter*, released in 2010, which coincidentally is when Marni and I first made contact.

What began as a simple interview about the stories that hold us back when it comes to clearing out clutter quickly blossomed into a professional kinship rooted in a mutual passion: helping people help themselves. Not only did Marni take my advice, she left no stone unturned.

Armed with "smelling salts and a bulldozer," Marni takes no prisoners in her quest to clear out her parents' homestead, keeping the items that truly matter and liquidating those that don't into the funds needed to sustain her parents in assisted living. Along with her humility and chutzpah, what becomes evidently clear is that she, like many of us— afraid of dishonoring our parents when making decisions about their personal items—proves that it can be done with respect, dignity, and, above all, their approval.

A sign of our times, *Downsizing the Family Home* is one of the most comprehensive resource books I've ever read about how to divvy the goods and allocate precious items in today's marketplace. Finally, direct answers to the impossible question: What do I keep, sell, donate, or trash? Providing readers with detailed instructions and valuable resources, Marni has emerged as more than an astute columnist and investigative reporter on all things home. She is a true advocate of the heart. And that, my friends, is why this book will serve you and generations to come.

Be prepared to laugh, cry, and let go. Then hold on tight to what matters most.

Enjoy!

MARK BRUNETZ

Introduction
But It Was Mom's!

All across the country, the groans are getting louder as the adult children of aging parents, and often the parents themselves, look at a lifetime of accumulations and cry: "What am I going to do with all this stuff?" Never before in history have we been blessed with so much—and felt so overwhelmed by it.

Although I now know that I am not alone, I sure felt alone in January 2013 when I stood paralyzed on the threshold of my childhood home, a fully loaded house where my parents had lived for nearly fifty years. I, too, cried, "What am I going to do with all this stuff?" as I faced the task of clearing out the old homestead and getting it on the market.

Waylaid by emotion and the responsibility for doing the right thing—whatever that was—with my parents' lifetime's worth of possessions, I felt ill equipped.

I wanted to be respectful of my parents' belongings, honor their lives, be a good steward of their assets, and preserve their past and mine. At the same time, I didn't want to be weighed down by more stuff, even if that stuff meant something—and it almost all did. I had a house full of things, too. Although I knew that most older parents, including mine, want to gift their children with the assets of their productive lives and bequeath them the roots of their history, they do not want their households to be albatrosses.

But the line between bestow and burden is blurry.

I looked for help and found little published about what to do with the avalanche that the greatest generation is leaving to those in its wake. The books I could find were written by estate-sale professionals, who approached a houseful of memories and stuff as a business problem, with the solution being to hire an expert. That seemed to be missing the heart of the matter. Many books also deal with clutter, but calling your parents' belongings clutter seems demeaning. We're dealing with a vast amount of memory-laden, historical,

© Marni Jameson

The house in Orange, California, my parents and I called home for nearly half a century.

occasionally valuable, often irreplaceable acquisitions. In short, we're talking about the museum of your family's life.

Faced with this, I did what I do. As a journalist and nationally syndicated columnist who has written a column on home life and home design for a dozen years, I called on my own pool of experts—antiques appraisers, organizing gurus, family psychologists, art experts, and garage-sale aficionados—and grilled them.

I applied the pieces of their advice that made sense to me along with my own instincts and wrote about it all as I went through the process. In my weekly column, I chronicled this rite of passage: the learning and loving and letting go.

Never in my nearly thirty years of writing for media had one topic struck such a chord. I received hundreds of e-mails from readers asking me to please put my columns in a book. Some shared their stories. Others asked my advice. One reader told me she'd kept all the columns and put them in her safe deposit box for her kids to read.

I was humbled, of course. And then I did what I do when I am trying to find answers: I wrote a book. It goes like this:

Almost every adult child someday will face a parent's mortality and, by extension, the contents of that parent's household. It's almost inescapable.

Although some adult children tackle the task of dismantling a parent's home after the parent's death, others face it when a parent downsizes into a home that is smaller and easier to manage or enters assisted living. Some adult children and their parents work together during this transition, discussing family lore and heritage as they sort. This is ideal but rare. Some older adults—also a minority—anticipate the job their kids will face and get a jump on clearing out their homes as a gift to their children. The majority cling to their belongings partly out of avoidance, partly out of emotional and physical inertia, and with the false belief that they can hand them down to the next generation (which doesn't really want them).

All this is happening against a backdrop of the greatest age of consumerism in U.S. history. After generations of relative scarcity and thrift, from the 1950s onward, this nation has experienced booming consumerism. A ready, steady supply of inexpensive household goods has filled homes— closets and cupboards, garages and sheds, attics and basements—to bursting. Our consumerism has inspired a whole industry. We now have professionals trained to help people bust their clutter and get organized; it has even spawned a national association of professional organizers. We have books and TV shows devoted to the problem of having and holding on to too much stuff.

Families used to have one radio, but they now have five televisions, one the size of a billboard. The single family-photo album is now box upon box of photos that no family can keep up with. Everyday goods that once were hard to come by—clothing, linens, dishes, tools—are now easy to get but still, for many, hard to let go of.

Add to prolific consumerism the facts that Americans are on average living longer and that the longer we live, the more we tend to have, and that older adults with very full houses often have adult children with their own very full houses . . . and, well, you can see the snowball effect that happens when one full house gets rolled into another. It's hard enough to manage our own household's belongings, but add a parent's, with its inherent memories, guilt, stories of worth, and the excruciating sentiment—"But it was Mom's!"—and it can be suffocating.

This generation-on-generation snowball is growing, and whether you are forty or one hundred, you are in its path. Every day, 8,000 Americans turn sixty-five, a trend that will continue until 2030. By then, one in five Americans will be eighty or older.

So what's the problem? It's just stuff, you say.

Here's the problem:

The family home is loaded in every sense. It's loaded not only with belongings, but also with memories. Most homes have items that can trip those clearing them out into sinkholes of sentiment. As the family museum, the old homestead is filled with relics that represent a lifetime of storied treasures: art collected during travels, dresses worn for special occasions, dining tables where grace was said and milestones celebrated, significant jewelry, military medals, family photos, yearbooks, and mounds of documents, important and not.

Sorting through it all is emotionally, mentally, and physically overwhelming. But if it is done right, I've learned, it can be tremendously rewarding.

In this book, I will take you on my journey of clearing out my elderly parents' home of nearly fifty years, from the moment I stood paralyzed on the threshold to the day it was sold to a new young family.

I also will share the downsizing that was occurring in my parallel life, when I moved from a large family home where I'd raised my children and re-created a new life in a smaller house, a newly single woman with a lot less stuff. Along the way I will share advice from others who have gone down their own roads to downsizing and the many experts I am fortunate enough to work with and call my friends.

These interviews, my midlife experience, and my parents' downsizing into assisted living made me reflect a lot on the meaning of home, family, memory, what matters, what to keep, what to turn into cash (and how), and what to let go of.

It's a tough balance, but this book will help you find it.

PART ONE

The Home Front

NOSTALGIA: A sentimental longing or wistful affection for the past, typically for a period or place with happy personal associations: from the Greek words *nostos*, "return home," and *algos*, "pain."

A Tough Call

How to Know When an Aging Parent Needs a New Home

"Things are only worth what you make them worth."

—MOLIÈRE

My brother and I had a plan for our aging parents. The plan was that they would not age. They would never need to move from the house where they had lived for forty-five years, the only childhood home I could remember.

They had a plan, too. They would manage just fine, thank you.

But as they both approached their ninetieth birthdays, their living situation grew rickety.

Mom took a few spills. Because she couldn't get up by herself and Dad couldn't lift her, he had to call the fire department twice and a neighbor once to help her get up. She was getting forgetful, and her clothes weren't as clean as they should have been.

Meanwhile, Dad was losing weight. When I asked him if that was because of his new dentures, or because he wasn't shopping, or because he didn't have the energy to fix meals, he said, "Yes." He got worn out just going out front to get the paper.

When he turned ninety, his driver's license would expire. He would have to stop driving, as he should. Their once-robust world, which had been so full of friends and church activities and places to be, had shrunk considerably over the last several years and was about to get even smaller.

My unwillingness to believe that my capable, independent parents were losing their hold did not prevent it from happening. My parents were heroes to me, and, actually, they were in fact heroes. They met in 1945 on Okinawa in Japan, where Mom, who was born in Scotland and grew up in Pennsylvania, was an army nurse, and Dad, a fourth-generation Californian, born and raised in Los Angeles, was a marine fighter pilot. They were brave and dashing. Dad proposed after three weeks. Mom held him off for three years, and then East met West in 1948 when they married and settled in Hollywood. Shortly afterward, Dad went off to Korea as a helicopter evacuation pilot while Mom finished her nursing degree at UCLA and started working as a public health nurse, "telling strange men they had syphilis," she used to say, at which point my eyebrows would rise.

After the war, Dad went to work as a hydraulics engineer, the mental force behind more than two dozen patents. After kids came along in the late 1950s and early 1960s, Mom worked as a school nurse and created a stable, love-filled home that was the center of our universe.

They had full lives, and I saw no reason for that to end.

See, when I was young, I believed that only about three in ten people really died. As I got older, I thought maybe that number was closer to seven in ten, but my immediate family would remain among the living. Death was for other people.

Now, seeing my parents at this stage, I started thinking the number might actually be close to ten in ten. This awareness might be what some call maturity.

Sensing the storm clouds on the horizon, my older, wiser brother, Craig, began the Talk. For almost a year, Craig, whom my parents had named executor for the family years earlier, had been trying to convince our parents—and me—that they would be much better off—safer, happier, healthier—in a home with some help.

Dad listened with his characteristic calibrated reason and logic.

Mom listened with her characteristic preformed opinion and dislike of change: "I'm sure these places are nice, but we're managing just fine, thank you."

To me, *we* was the operative word. As long as they had each other, they had a cross-check in place—tenuous though it was. Dad's vision was poor, and so Mom distributed the pills. When Mom fell, Dad got her up even if he had to call in reinforcements. It somehow worked, if a bit precariously.

"What will happen when one of them goes first?" Craig asked me.

"What do you mean when one of them goes?" I said, sounding like Mom and thinking that our parents would be among those, in my calculation, who defied death.

"We would have to instantly move the other one into assisted living, and that would be more traumatic. It would be better to move them together," he said.

"What about their domestic routines?" I asked. He makes the coffee; she pours the cereal. He makes the bed; she folds the laundry. They take their tea on the patio and watch the birds at the feeder.

"What about their safety and meals and socializing?"

CRAIG TOOK DAD to see some assisted-living centers around town. Dad warmed to the idea of a social life, prepared meals, and no house and yard to maintain. They weighed factors such as proximity to church and doctors, cost, levels of care, and vibe. Some centers felt like country clubs; others looked so downtrodden that Craig and Dad didn't get beyond the parking lot.

After a few field trips, they found a center that felt as right as one could feel. The residents and staff seemed happy. The place had beautiful grounds, a gym, a nice dining room, and an available corner apartment that over-looked the well-kept gardens. They could furnish it with their things, albeit a small collection, which I knew would go a long way toward buffering the blow, but a blow it would be to all of us nonetheless.

They brought Mom out and had lunch there.

"This is nice, but we're managing just fine, thank you," she declared.

"I put a deposit down," Dad told me.

"How do you feel about that?" I asked.

"Queasy," he said.

"Me, too."

"We're going to try it for a couple of months," he told Mom. He'd been telling her for weeks about this plan, repeating it often because she'd forget, and who could blame her?

"But we're managing just fine."

"No one's selling the house," he assured her, which was true at least at that moment, though it was in the cards for later. "We can always come back," which was probably not true.

"But we're managing just fine," she said. "Aren't we?"

THOUGH FAMILY DYNAMICS DIFFER, all across the nation similar conversations are taking place as the boomer generation takes care of the Greatest Generation, and Gen Xers step up to care for older boomers, the front wave of whom are hitting their seventies. In some situations, older parents are proactively downsizing homes to lighten the eventual load on their offspring.

What everyone in the mix eventually realizes is that if parents live long enough, the time inevitably comes when they must pass the baton—and all that goes with it—to their adult children. Although that natural progression is as old as time, when the seesaw tilts from parent to adult child, all parties feel they are facing a new frontier. And they are.

Deciding it's time to move a parent from his or her home of many years to assisted living is among the toughest decisions adult children can make. Avoiding the decision or ignoring the issues isn't in a parent's best interest.

Ideally, older adults make this decision on their own or in collaboration with their children. Some require an intervention. In our case, Mom and Dad were split. But the fact that Dad saw the need and wanted to proceed helped us work with Mom's resistance.

Even so, a part of me, the wishful irrational part, wasn't convinced she was wrong. I certainly would have liked to see my parents age in place. Mom, who was Scottish, as I previously mentioned, identified herself and the rest of the McCormack clan as "the bulldog breed." She often said, "We McCormacks die in the trenches," meaning they stayed put.

But as I did my research, I found a clear set of criteria outlining when it's time to move a parent. Such evaluations require a cool head and a clear unblinking look at issues of safety, health, hygiene, housekeeping, meals, and social life. Craig already had done the analysis and was waiting for me.

As I evaluated whether this move was right for my elderly parents, I had to check every box:

- *Safety.* If they've had falls, driving mishaps, or bruises or cuts they'd rather you not know about, more support is in their best interest.
- *Health.* Failing eyesight, poor balance, forgetfulness, low stamina, poor health, and a combination of these issues are indications that a parent will benefit from more assistance in daily living.
- *Hygiene.* A change in hygiene habits is often a sign that parents need help—the kind they are unlikely to ask for. If you notice that your formerly impeccably dressed parent is wearing the same clothes over and over and not noticing when they're dirty, or if he or she is beginning to have an odor, gently suggest that they may need some help with their daily personal care.

(So far I was three for three.)

- *Housekeeping.* If their dishes and laundry are not getting done, the corners of their home have cobwebs, and the housework in their previously well-managed place is sliding, living on their own may be neither hygienic nor safe.

- *Meals.* If they're losing weight, are not getting to the grocery store, or have spoiled food in the refrigerator, a place that provides regular balanced meals could greatly enhance and sustain their lives.
- *Social life.* As people age, their circle of friends often diminishes. My parents' once bustling social life had dwindled to the point where they rarely got out. A good assisted-living (or even independent-living) center can offer stimulation and social activities that can improve quality of life and mental well-being.

As my parents often said, the right choice and the easy choice are rarely the same.

When my brother and I reviewed this situation together, we knew what we had to do. Dad did, too.

Of course, other older adults may not need the level of care my parents did, and will do well moving from a larger family home into a smaller, easier-to-maintain home or a one-floor town home.

Other times, a sudden passing leaves no time for a transition to a smaller place.

Whatever the circumstances—whether parents are downsizing to enjoy a more carefree, lower-maintenance lifestyle or to lighten the load on their children, or if they need more support and assistance in their daily living, or if adult children are intervening out of need or because of a parent's passing—a houseful of stuff and memories needs to be sorted out.

Get ready for double-black-diamond terrain.

TAKEAWAY

When parents need to move from their longtime home into smaller quarters or an assisted-living center, the path is neither clear nor smooth. Adult children often need to take the reins.

2

Get the Right Mind-Set

Facing the Fully Loaded House

> *"Our house was not unsentient matter—it had a heart and a soul, and eyes to see with. . . . We never came home from an absence that its face did not light up and speak out its eloquent welcome—and we could not enter it unmoved."*
>
> —MARK TWAIN

My brother and his wife, whom we call Chickie, coordinated the move from my parents' home to their new assisted-living apartment. They worked with a company with expertise in these types of moves to select what should go (and would fit) and what needed to stay behind and ran it by me to make double sure, as if anyone could be sure.

We tagged their bedroom furniture, complete with the dresser and its accompanying family photos, which we would arrange in exactly the same way; their favorite blue sitting chairs and coffee table; a small kitchen table and two chairs; clothes relevant to their current stage of life; and several pieces of artwork. But 90 percent of their belongings stayed behind in the house they had lived in for nearly half a century.

Chickie took Mom out for lunch and shopping while Craig and Dad supervised the move. I sat on the opposite coast, 3,000 miles away, my stomach producing hydrochloric acid by the gallon.

When they brought Mom to her new place, she made two fists, closed her eyes, and shook her head, and said, "No, no, no." That was rough.

My brother sent me videos of the new place. It was heartbreakingly heartening, a sort of comforting shock if that's possible, to see their furnishings lovingly assembled in a new, safer place.

Several months later, after Mom and Dad had settled into their new quarters and grown accustomed to having three hot meals a day in the dining room, Dad told me to "do whatever you need to do" with their household belongings, with the goal of clearing the house out and selling it. He would rest easier—and to put it frankly, he later did die in peace—if this asset (the house plus all its contents) was liquidated and the proceeds were easily accessible to pay for their long-term care.

Because Craig, as the executor, had taken on the huge task of managing my parents' finances, including healthcare affairs, and coordinating the move to assisted living, and because I am the so-called home expert, the task of clearing out and selling the house fell squarely on me. Quite honestly, I wanted to do it.

And I wanted to do it really well.

Therefore, at my father's request, I embarked on the

task of emptying the fully loaded four-bedroom, two-bath house, updating it, and getting it ready to be put on the market. "Whatever you need to do" were his words, though I honestly wasn't at all sure what that entailed.

RESEARCH MODE—EVALUATING THE OPTIONS

As I started to think about how to tackle this monster project, I did what journalists do: I researched. In my nearly thirty years as a reporter, including more than a decade as a syndicated home-design columnist, I had made a lot of contacts, and I wasn't shy about using them.

I needed information, a strategy, and an efficient game plan. My parents' home was in California, and I lived in Florida. I had a teenager in high school and a full-time newspaper job, and so I had to be realistic about how much time I could devote to this task.

Fortunately, the angels of timing smiled down on me. Just as I was in the first stages of paralysis (a recurring sensation over the next two months) and was feeling defeated by the size of the job before I'd even started, help arrived.

As if in answer to my cry to the universe—"Help! I have to clear out my elderly parents' stuffed-full house, and I don't know what to do with it all!"—my friend Aaron LaPedis, author of *The Garage Sale Millionaire* and host of the PBS program of the same name, came to town. I'd interviewed Aaron, who lives in Denver, for my column several times over the years. He e-mailed to let me know he had come to my town, Orlando, to visit the theme parks with his wife and his three-year-old son. I took this happy coincidence for what it was: divine deliverance.

Sure enough, Aaron graciously agreed to interrupt his adventures to squeeze in coffee with me.

He swore he didn't mind listening to me blubber about my home-life problems when he could be meeting princesses at Epcot.

Aaron has made houses full of stuff his business. He is just as at home at a high-end antiques auction as he is at a low-end yard sale. Though I wasn't sure, I thought my parents' stuff fell into both categories. Aaron also gets markets and sees opportunities that others can't.

"Can I just channel you for the next few months?" I asked.

"You can do this," he said, a one-man pep squad.

Then I laid out the million-dollar question: "How do you know what to toss and what to keep, and what to sell and where to sell and for how much?" That was all. Could he please just answer that?

That was what I needed to know as I prepared myself for the job ahead, I told him. Not just the disposition of furniture but also the sifting and sorting through Mom's jewelry and Dad's tools; their art, dishes, collections, linens, clothing, letters, photos, and locks from first haircuts; and hundreds, perhaps thousands, of random objects that once meant something—if only to them.

By then I was ranting and working myself into a state of panic. When I paused to breathe, Aaron said in summary: "So you want to liquidate."

As men have a knack for doing, he changed everything in a word.

Liquidate.

"That's it!" I said. "I've been thinking about this all wrong. I've had it in my mind that I'm erasing their history—our history—that I am destroying the family museum, writing the final chapter to a bygone era . . . when I'm just liquidating! Selling assets to help pay for their long-term assisted living." (And, perhaps, preserving a few treasures and a little legacy for myself, and my children, and maybe their children.)

Lightbulbs were flashing in my brain like paparazzi's cameras. The pure obviousness was dawning on me. "I'm being sentimental when I need to be practical. You've helped me reframe everything!"

He looked at me as if I needed a tranquilizer and nodded politely.

"A lot of people are turning stuff they don't want into cash for other reasons, including downsizing," he said.

"I'm liquidating, not erasing history!"

Later I will share Aaron's golden advice on what to sell where, including what to sell at a garage or estate sale, on Craigslist® or eBay®, at auction or in a consignment store, but the first lesson was this: More than anything else, what I needed—and what you will need whether you're downsizing your own house or a loved one's—was the right mind-set.

I needed a mental filter through which to look at the household's stuff and all the associated memories to help me sort swiftly and decisively. I needed a divining rod to guide me through the process in a way that let me honor the past and not burden the future, and which allowed me to be a respectful steward of my parents' belongings and our family history—not a sappy sentimentalist who can't let go.

TAKEAWAY

When downsizing the family home, take care not to let sentiment be your governor. Stay focused on your goal— clear out and liquidating—and hold the rudder steady.

3

Endowment

Why We Get So Attached to Things

"Home is a name, a word, it is a strong one; stronger than magician ever spoke, or spirit ever answered to, in the strongest conjuration."

—CHARLES DICKENS

I had made my plans to travel to California in two weeks. Meanwhile, I was still doing my reconnaissance so that I would have some direction when I hit what I came to call the home front. What I kept hearing when I asked experts in the business of selling estates was not so much the specifics of how to know what's valuable but a big fat warning about the emotional toll that lay before me.

Here's why. Simply and starkly put, sorting through a household makes us face our own mortality: the passage of time, life and death, where we've been, where we haven't been, where we are in life, successes and regrets.

That's enough to give even the most hard-hearted human permanent pause.

For more clarity and more than a little therapy, I called

my friend and organizing guru Peter Walsh, host of TLC's *Clean Sweep*, who happened to be going through this process with his own mother. I asked him why a parent's household is so emotionally charged.

"Because this isn't about the stuff," he said. "This is about dealing with fundamental issues of families and growth and loss and love."

"How can you deal with that?"

"Know what you're about to step into," he said. "Before you ever step into the room with the items, psychologically brace yourself for a shock. You're going to feel as if you're plunging into icy water. As you're going under, expect that you will be breathless at some stage."

"Good to know," I said, and felt my spine stiffen. Then he told me why that was.

"Everything we own has power," Peter said. "Letting go of anything we have seen or used or experienced as a child is hard because the memory embedded in the object has such power. We fear if we let go of the object, we'll lose the memory."

We also have to be prepared to face the facts that life is fleeting and that we lose our parents, he said. Clearing out or downsizing a home, whether a parent's or our own, is a rite of passage that is significant and painful and traumatic.

"Am I deluding myself to think I can do this sanely, strategically, respectfully, and rewardingly while striking the right balance of pragmatism, economy, good stewardship, and heart?"

"You absolutely can," he assured me.

Then, as a cautionary tale, Peter shared an experience he'd had with a couple. The husband had lost his mother and put all her stuff in the couple's garage. He said he could really use Peter's help. "Every time I walk through the garage, I am so overwhelmed by all the things from her home that were so important to her and by the sense of loss and her passing," he said. "I just can't bring myself to clear the stuff out."

"How long ago did she die?" Peter asked.

"Eighteen months," the man said.

"Four years," the wife corrected.

That said it all.

I was not going to be that man.

PUTTING THE PAST IN PERSPECTIVE

Before we go any further, let's talk for a moment about attachment, specifically, why we get so attached to stuff.

Mark Brunetz, cohost of Style Network's *Clean House*, who kindly wrote the foreword to this book, was the first to share with me the concept of *endowment*, a term psychologists use to describe our relationship with our things. The minute we acquire any item, whether we buy it or find it, whether it's a gift or inherited, it will never again be neutral.

It's endowed with all that came with it: the store or town where you bought it, the occasion, the person who gave it to you. The item can conjure good or bad feelings, mild or intense, but it will never be neutral. It carries an emotional charge. Knowing and understanding that everything has a story can actually help you detach yourself from that item.

"It's not the stuff we have to deal with; it's the stories behind the stuff," Mark is known for saying.

When the belongings we're encountering are those of a parent, spouse, or child, they are even more charged, especially if the loved one is gone, he said.

It also helps to understand that attachment is normal and healthy in humans, said Dr. Daniel Bober, a psychiatrist and assistant clinical professor at Yale School of Medicine. Attachments start very early. Think of an infant who gets attached to a parent or caretaker and then transfers the good warm feelings to a blanket or stuffed animal he or she associates with that comfort and security. Adults make similar transfers to objects that they endow with meaning; a wedding ring is one of the most powerful.

When we lose someone dear and go through his or her stuff, it's painful because these objects get merged with the person and then further remind us that everything in life is temporary, explained Dr. Bober. "That makes us want to hang on to these objects."

To help yourself let go, tell yourself that the important attachment is not to any object but to the person the object represents. "Whether you keep the object or let it go doesn't change your connection to a loved one," he said.

TAKEAWAY

Children often form attachments to transitional objects, such as blankets and teddy bears, that remind them of the warmth and security they get from a parent or caretaker. The feelings adults have for their parents' possessions also evoke the comfort and affection they received from their parents, and that makes letting go extra hard.

4

The First Cut

Going Through It Together

"There is no use in loving things if you have to be torn from them, is there? And it's so hard to keep from loving things, isn't it?"

—L. M. MONTGOMERY

It was a small consolation that five years before my parents moved into their assisted-living apartment, I had taken a run at clearing out the home with Mom. At that time, Mom and Dad were in their mideighties, and the stuff in the home where they had lived for four-plus decades had gotten the upper hand.

Though I didn't know at the time how long they would stay in their home (maybe forever?), I knew it needed a major purge, and that wasn't going to happen unless I did it with them. Though they both, thank goodness, still had their wits, they were frail. Mom's balance wasn't great; Dad ran out of air. But something had to be done about the closets before an avalanche crushed them.

Dad was all for it, but Mom has always preferred the status quo to just about anything.

I had been telling Mom for over a month that I was going to fly in for a visit and work with her and Dad to clean out some of the clutter that was building up in their home. But when the day arrived, the idea still came as a shock to Mom.

"This just hit me so fast," Mom said over the phone the night before my flight. Her anxiety tremors were registering 8.0 on the Richter scale.

"Mom, we've been discussing this for weeks." Judging by her enthusiasm, you'd think I was coming to personally extract all her teeth.

"But I may not agree with you."

"We're not going to throw away anything you still want."

"I'm sentimental."

"We're simplifying your life, not erasing your past."

I heard a long train of steam exit her nostrils, a familiar sound that I knew meant she was teetering between resistance and resignation.

"The problem with this house is that I have no storage space," Mom said as we hit the first closet.

"You will when I'm done," I said. "What's in here?"

"Miscellaneous."

"And here?"

"More miscellaneous."

MY GOAL WAS THREE CLOSETS IN TWO DAYS: their bedroom closet, the den closet, and the guest-room closet. Mom had clothes in all three. Some garments she hadn't worn in fifty years, and many were from days when she was thirty pounds heavier.

"Have you seen yourself?" I asked, holding up a top that would fit two of her. She had outfits with oversized shoulder pads from the 1980s, when it was fashionable for women to look like armadillos; shoes with three-inch heels she couldn't walk in today; and . . . what was this? Old maternity clothes?

"I'm all for medical miracles, Mom, but seriously?"

"I thought they'd make nice drapes."

We found bundles of Christmas cards saved by year going back to William the Conqueror.

"Out?" she guessed.

"Mom, they are greeting cards. Their job is to greet you over the holidays. They did that. Now, you throw them away."

We put the cards in the toss pile, along with a reel-to-reel tape recorder that weighed as much as a sewing machine, a wooden recipe box stuffed with grocery coupons that had expired in 1996, boxes inside boxes filled with bows from every present she'd received since Watergate, and enough baskets to re-create the miracle of the loaves and fishes.

"They're good boxes," she said. "And I put cookies in the baskets to give to people."

"But you don't need fifty." We agreed to whittle the collections to five boxes and ten baskets.

From time to time, Dad would appear in the background,

grin, point two thumbs up, and then go back to making himself scarce.

"Oh, look, a dead badger," I said, pulling something furry from a box.

"Wigs were in style once."

"Why get one laced with gray?"

"I wanted to look natural."

I didn't mention that wrinkles were natural but you don't go out of your way to acquire them, and instead asked the key question: "Will you use it?"

"We sometimes pass it around at parties, and the men try it on."

I decided that was hilarious, and we kept the wig.

AFTER TWO DAYS, we filled several trash and recycle bins and half of the two-car garage for a thrift store pickup. As Mom collapsed in a chair with a bag of frozen peas over her eyes, Dad surveyed the mound. "I've been trying to get rid of this stuff for forty years," he said. "How'd you do it?"

"I just gave back what you guys gave me: unequivocal love and an occasional kick in the behind." Actually, pulling teeth might have been easier.

We made a good dent that weekend, but I wish I—and, frankly, they—had done a lot more before it had come to this.

GUIDING LIGHTS FOR SORTING

As I sorted through my parents' belongings, I applied organizing methods I've adopted over the years as a lifestyle and
home-design columnist and also during my four-year stint
as a live-in home stager, which I will tell you more about
later. But for now, just know that my closets and cupboards
had to be orderly and clutter-free at all times.

I also am someone who aspires to live well and beautifully, and so I really do try to put these methods into practice in my own home. The experience of doing this with
Mom was good practice and gave me a running start for
when I tackled the much larger task of clearing out the
home several years later. These tips were my guiding lights
then and now. They have become a way of living:

- *When sorting, ask these questions:* Do I love
  it? Do I need it? Will I use it? If you don't
  answer yes to one of them, the item goes. The
  following rationales—in the absence of at least
  one yes—are not reasons for hanging on: But I
  only wore it once. It's still in good condition. It
  was expensive. But so-and-so gave it to me.
- *Divide and conquer.* Tackle one area at a
  time: a closet, a room, a pantry. As you gain
  control over one space, you feel encouraged
  to take on the next one, and you see the

progress. Pulling several areas apart at once probably will be too overwhelming.

- *Choose to keep rather than choose to let go.* When you are cleaning a closet, rather than moving through the items and deciding what to eliminate, do the reverse. Take everything out, down to the bare walls. Then physically put back the items you choose to keep. That process makes you choose to keep rather than choose to let go and will result in your clinging to fewer things.

- *Don't put it off.* Procrastination is the root of all clutter. Now is better than later. When you play kick the can down the road, guess what? The problem always gets bigger. Purge regularly and often.

- *Unpack your stories.* In the hours we've spent talking over the years, Mark Brunetz really showed me how, as previously mentioned, that it is not about the stuff, it's about the stories behind the stuff. Once you understand the stories, you can manage the emotions better and make practical decisions to let go. Here are the most common stories:

1. **I'D FEEL GUILTY IF I GOT RID OF THAT.**
   Guilt is not a reason to hoard. For instance, say you have a dining-room table your

parents gave you, but it's just not working
in your home. Understand and accept that
what worked for your parents' lives doesn't
necessarily work for yours.

2. **I MIGHT NEED THAT SOMEDAY.** Living
   your life for one day in the future robs you of
   today. We need to live in the present. When
   we project life into either the past or the
   future, we eclipse the now.

3. **IT HAS SENTIMENTAL VALUE.** "How you
   love someone lives in your heart, not in your
   home," Mark said. "Your heart can never be
   too full, but your home can be. The love you
   have for a grandparent or a sibling doesn't
   live in an inanimate object."

- *Sentiment is okay, within reason.* "I'm not saying
  get rid of all your stories," Mark said. "Strike
  a middle ground. Keep what you're attached
  to, but only if it's not encumbering you. And
  yes, you can have the occasional sentimental
  item." Mark has his great-grandfather's
  engraved mahogany humidor in his living
  room. Though he doesn't smoke or store
  cigars, "it reminds me where I came from
  and where I'm going. The humidor is from a
  man who spent his professional life as a master
  wallpaper hanger. It reminds me that I am a

fourth-generation artisan, the descendant of a man who climbed up on a ladder day after day to make something more beautiful."

- *Play it out.* When you're tempted to hang on to something, ask yourself what will become of this item in ten years if you hang on to it. Will it bestow a benefit or be a burden? This is especially true if you have adult children, who no doubt will have their own fully loaded homes when they're in a position to sort through your things. Even if you aren't planning to leave this earth any time soon, get rid of your albatrosses now. Wonderful families help each other across generations. I know this is touchy territory, but think beyond what your stuff means to you and consider how it will affect others. Be sensitive enough, wise enough, and giving enough to cut it down.

- *Do it together.* If practical, older parents and adult children should sort, purge, and save together so stories can be passed down. But if getting together is not easy, don't make that an excuse to put off the job. Often, children wait until their parents move out or move on to do this work and find themselves wishing one of the parents were around to ask about the stories.

Doing the housekeeping when we did let my parents reclaim quality space, enjoy a better-functioning home, and share their stories as we sorted. The more parents can do this up front or can work with their grown kids to do it, the easier this task will be in the long run. Looking back, I wish we had done more.

> ### TAKEAWAY
>
> A key message of this book is that editing and paring a lifetime of memories is not something to put off until you approach or cross life's finish line. Rather, make sorting and selling and clearing out what you no longer need or use or love a way of living. It will make your life better now and lighten the burden on you and eventually on your loved ones.

5

Welcome to the Home Front

A Blast from the Past

"Take time to deliberate, but when the time for action comes, stop thinking and go in."

—NAPOLEON BONAPARTE

Fast-forward five years.

Armed with some idea—partly thanks to Aaron LaPedis, Peter Walsh, and Mark Brunetz—of how to attack the old homestead, I took a week off from my newspaper job in Orlando and parachuted into Orange, California, landing at the door of my childhood home.

Welcome to the home front.

I knew one long week (nine days including weekends) would not be time enough to clear out nearly half a century of living in one house and more than sixty years of marriage; not time enough to sort through the mountains of memorabilia that had accrued, the dishes and documents, linens and letters, crystal and cookware, photos and furniture, tools and trinkets.

But a week was what I had.

I had a teenage daughter back home staying with friends

while I was away, and I didn't want to put her or them out longer than that. Also, I could not afford to take more than a week off from work.

Because I also believe that a task will expand or contract to fill the amount of time you have, I figured allowing myself a week for a job that could easily take the rest of my life would provide some boundaries.

I knew it would be hard work mentally, emotionally, and physically. My goal was to have the home emptied to the point where crews could come in and paint and make improvements to ready it for sale.

All that steel-willed practicality melted and ran out of my little toe once I stepped over the threshold into the only childhood home I'd ever known. I knew every inch of the 1,800-square-foot, single-story ranch with its pitched roof, long eaves, and pale-yellow wood siding. I knew every tree and bush in the yard, and there wasn't a window in the house I hadn't climbed through. For me, the house was the source of life's essentials: unconditional love, good advice, a clean bed, a moral compass, hot coffee, and sustenance of every kind. It was a home I returned to often with my own children, who had my mother's cookies and milk at the same counter I did, played in the same yard, and climbed the same tree.

Struck by the cascade of memories, I stood paralyzed in the entry as if I'd suddenly grown roots. To get through my job here, I realized, I'd need smelling salts and a bulldozer.

It was the first time I'd been inside the home since my

brother and sister-in-law, with the help of movers, had relocated my parents to their new quarters. The house seemed cruelly empty without Mom and Dad there.

The home looked much the same, though missing were the few items of furniture, pieces of art, and clothes that had gone with them to outfit their apartment at the assisted-living center. Without my parents there, the home felt hollow. What remained looked like a balloon bouquet with all the air let out.

When I finally untethered my feet and walked through the rooms to assess the scene, I discovered that it is possible to drown in sentiment.

As I stood in the home's various doorways, familiar smells hung in the air—my mother's ubiquitous L'Air du Temps® perfume and something like wool, which reminded me of Dad—seemingly ingrained in the dated floral wallpaper and damask drapes.

There was the scar on the bathroom Formica®, where my teenage self had left a cone of incense burning. Mom had smoothed it all over with a flower sticker. Thumbtack marks remained on the walls of my electric guitar–playing brother's old room. He had papered his room with black-light posters, causing Mom to jokingly refer to it as the den of iniquity.

At the base of the back screen door were scratch marks from where a steady stream of family dogs, all really Dad's dogs, had asked to go out.

I kept walking through the rooms, because if I stood still, moving again was nearly impossible.

Shake it off. It's just a house. It's only stuff. Easy to say.

However, if I'd learned anything during my own upheavals, it's that nothing busts a bout of self-pity like getting good and busy.

Because it was past midnight early Saturday morning in California when I crossed the threshold and after 3 a.m. eastern time, I decided to get some sleep and start fresh in the morning. I crashed in my old room. On the wall, a triangle from where my high school pennant once hung had ghosted into the faded yellow paint.

The next morning, bolstered by the three-hour time change, I charged in. As I do with any big project, I took a divide-and-conquer approach, breaking the task down into more manageable (I use that term very loosely) steps.

I started by surveying the contents of each room and cupboard and mentally began sorting stuff into categories, which felt callous but necessary: toss, donate, sell, keep, can't decide/can't bear to look at.

I thought of the Roman god Janus, who, like my parents, had eyes in the back of his head. In fact, he had an entire face on the back of his head, and so he could look backward and forward at once. That feature earned him the title "God of Doors." He ruled comings and goings.

I wanted some Janus juice just then. Specifically, I wanted to know what from the past I would want in the future. Come to think of it, I could also use the powers of Minerva, goddess of wisdom; Vesta, goddess of the home; and, for sure, Bacchus, god of wine.

Because Janus didn't answer my call, I phoned Miller Gaffney, one of the hosts of PBS's *Market Warriors* and a Sotheby's-trained art and antiques appraiser. "I don't know where to start," I said.

"You're not alone," she assured me. "A lot of downsizing is going on right now. Lots of people are sorting and selling."

Then she and I put together the following pointers for me and anyone else about to clean out an elder's attic, basement, garage, or home:

- *Make rough cuts.* As you sift through a household of belongings and memories, separate items into categories: toss, sell (or donate), keep, and can't decide. To avoid losing momentum, remember that these are preliminary cuts. No decision is permanent yet. In the toss pile, put items that make you say, Good Lord, why would anybody want this? (Don't toss them yet. You may be surprised.) In the sell pile, separate what may be valuable from plain stuff. For now, put the items you plan to donate in the sell pile. If they don't sell at an estate sale, you can donate them. In the keep area, park any items that make you say, "I don't care what it's worth, I'm keeping it." (We'll talk about this in Chapter 6.)

- *Do some homework.* One of the biggest concerns people have when downsizing or clearing out a house is that they are going to overlook something valuable, that they might sell a painting at a garage sale for $15 that the buyer later sells at an art auction for $50,000. We will discuss the value of things in Chapter 7 and what art is worth in Chapter 8, but I will start by saying—and please sit down—that the chances of your having something really valuable are pretty low. Unless you come from a very wealthy family, your belongings—even the "antiques"—are worth less than you think, at least money-wise. That is both a bummer and a blessing.
- *Get the scoop.* Parents tell your children and children ask your parents what is valuable or what is believed to be valuable. Share or ask for the history and sales records of potentially worthy items.
- *Be skeptical of the family legend.* That said, understand that heirlooms have a way of gathering unwarranted value as their legend grows. A friend told me about a Tiffany® lamp her grandmother cherished and said was worth a mint. An appraiser delivered the bad news: The lamp was a fake. In other words, don't believe everything Grandma said.

- *Don't do it alone.* Once you've separated out what might have value (furniture, jewelry, artwork, porcelain, other collectibles), ask a certified appraiser to do a walk-through inspection with you and identify items worth a closer look. Then get those items appraised. (We'll talk more about how to find an appraiser and how to self-appraise in Chapter 7.)

- *Realize it's not worth it.* Just as that piece of junk you thought was worthless could be a hidden treasure, more often than not, the items that family members believe have value don't. For instance, almost no market exists for figurines, and this often disappoints those who've collected them. Signed and numbered prints also don't usually fetch what the owners paid unless the artist became well-known, Miller said.

- *Decide what to keep.* Tougher than deciding what to toss or sell is deciding— selectively—what to keep. We will discuss this at length throughout this book, but Miller's top-line advice is this: When keeping an item for your home, consider condition, quality, whether the piece has an aesthetically pleasing shape, and how difficult it would be to ship. Beyond that, determining what to keep is a highly personal decision. "Some people don't want any reminders and just want to liquidate. Some just want the cookie jar. But others have a strong emotional connection to many furnishings," she said. You have to find your sweet spot and figure out how that fits in with what other family members might want.

TAKEAWAY

Do your homework and sort with care. Though the chances are slim that you will have anything truly valuable, if you have a question about an heirloom, get an expert opinion. You don't want to give away that ugly painting only to find out it sold for $50,000 later at an auction.

6

Plan E for Estate Sale

For Sale: Fifty Years of Treasures!

"We shape our dwellings, and afterwards our dwellings shape us."

—WINSTON CHURCHILL

As I mentioned in Chapter 1, my plan A was to let my parents live forever in their home, the way it had always been.

That didn't work. Plan B was to have my parents sort through all their stuff, downsize, sell, distribute heirlooms—or at least find out who would like what—and specify who would get cherished furnishings. Though that option is still available for many families (we'll see a good, real-world example of this when you meet the Switzes in Chapter 17), it was too late for mine.

Plan C was to seal up the house like a time capsule, preserving memories in a sort of shrine. That was tempting. Believe me, I would have liked to have locked the door and left the home as it was forever, but I knew that was only crazy talk.

Plan D was to pack up everything and save it or store it

somewhere else until I could face it, which would be never. That was also tempting, but if you are considering this option, let me talk you off that ledge right now.

The thought of saving everything or almost everything in your garage or a storage locker or in your own home is a terrible idea. It is impractical, lazy, and expensive.

That leaves us with plan E. You must go through the house and pare it down or clear it out. That means you must part with things laden with meaningful memories, but not all of them.

You must figure out a way to look at your household or your parents' household and let go of what does not belong in your future. I am not saying it will be easy. I am saying I have been down this path and can light your way.

BACK AT THE HOME FRONT, I worked through one room at a time. I tried to move swiftly and not fall into sinkholes of sentiment. I kept sorting items into mounds: toss, sell, keep, unsure. The unsure pile grew faster than did any other. I got derailed often, sucked in by finds such as the suitcase containing Mom's wedding dress.

When I got too overwhelmed in one area, I left it for another. There were times I roamed from room to room looking for a task I could tackle emotionally as well as physically but couldn't find one.

Still, I steamrolled along, because it was Sunday and the painters were coming in four days, and everything in the house had to be gone or in the garage by then. If you're ever frozen in a sad well of pity, just schedule the painters.

I discovered, among other stashed secrets, that my British mother had enough crocheted doilies, dresser scarves, embroidered hankies, and linen tablecloths to cover the surface of the moon.

As the sale pile grew, I realized that to honor my parents' possessions and not just donate them all—which would be easier and had crossed my mind, believe me—I had to hold a garage sale, or, technically, an estate sale, as the bigger ones are called when entire households are involved. Because of my limited time in town and the fact that the painters were arriving on Thursday, I couldn't host a garage sale on Saturday, prime garage sale day, or so I thought. It was already Sunday. I would have to host the sale on two weekdays, in this case, Tuesday and Wednesday. I was worried that no one would come.

Boy, was I wrong. I later learned that in fact the best buyers—collectors and dealers and "professional pickers" who shop estate sales for a living—shop on weekdays.

My sister-in-law, Chickie, posted an ad on Craigslist, Estatesales.com, and PennySaver online. On Monday morning, after I spent a solid day emptying closets, drawers, and cupboards and sorting their contents, Craig and Chickie showed up at the house like angels to help set up for the sale. We corralled like items on display tables, putting similar categories together: purses, knickknacks, china, vases, books, CDs, floral arrangements, clothes, and figurines. Eventually, we turned the 1,800-square-foot house into a boutique.

The next morning I was up at 5 a.m., putting price stickers on items—$1, $5, $50, "Make an Offer." I put "Not for Sale" sticky notes on furniture I couldn't bear to sell, though I knew I should. I was making game-time decisions I didn't feel nearly qualified to make. I had a four-alarm headache.

INSIDE TIP: Though I had no clue what much of this stuff was worth, if anything, I took a stab at pricing by using this formula: what the item would cost in a secondhand store minus what I would pay someone to take it.

Chickie made signs—"GIANT ESTATE SALE—50 YEARS OF TREASURES"—and stuck them up around the neighborhood and near freeway exits and major intersections. She wrapped the signs in plastic because rain was coming, which I worried would dampen our turnout further.

TWO DAYS, ONE LIFETIME OF LESSONS

On the first day of the sale, although it was advertised to start at 8 a.m., by 7 a.m. a line had started forming at the front door. Here I was worried that no one would show up, and throngs of buyers were queuing up, making a numbered list of who was first, second, and so on. They clearly knew game rules I didn't. First come, first in, first dibs. When I peeked out, someone asked if I had a list for them to sign. I did not. I had to ask, *Should I?*

Yes. Apparently that, too, was the protocol. (The names and phone numbers would come in handy.)

We opened the doors to a rush of buyers followed by a steady stream of shoppers that lasted nearly two days. They came armed with magnifying glasses, penlights, and laptops, and queried their cell phones often. So it was that I learned firsthand the following lessons about secondhand sales:

- *Don't assume you can guess what people will buy.* A box of old rags, cans of rusty nails, an old meat grinder (to turn into a lamp), vintage postcards—all sold. The dustpan, broom, mop, and bucket sold. One couple bought the gallon jugs of bleach and white vinegar.
- *Nothing is sacred.* Expect to be invaded. Signs on doors that say "Don't Open" mean nothing. When getting ready for the estate sale, I had put trash in the driveway, donations in the garage, items for sale in the house, and what I wanted to keep away from buyers in the back bedroom with the door closed. Then shoppers came through like a blender and swirled it all together. One shopper took the single bath towel I was using from the bathroom even though I had

closed the bathroom door and put an "Off Limits" sign on it. Another asked how much for my blow-dryer, which was in the off-limits bathroom. Seriously, if you ever want to clear out a house, label everything "Off Limits," "Trash," or "Donation." Those are the items that will go first.

- *Weekdays are okay.* Weekend sales may attract more buyers, but midweek sales attract better buyers. Collectors, dealers, and professional pickers, who buy and sell for a living, typically shop during the workweek.
- *Some people have no class.* One buyer picked up a pile of old towels marked to sell for $1 each. She wanted the stack of roughly 15 towels for $5 to use in a rehabilitation center, she said. As Chickie finalized the sale, she found that the customer had shoved a few more treasures inside the stack.
- *Some people have a lot of class.* One collector customer pointed out that an all-white porcelain figurine I had priced at $5 was an unusual, first-issue Hummel®, circa 1939–45, before Hummels were painted. Judging by the stamp, it was probably worth closer to $1,500. He suggested that I reconsider the price.

ESTATE, GARAGE, YARD, RUMMAGE SALE: WHAT'S THE DIFFERENCE?

These terms often get blurred. Though the word *estate* conjures the image of an expansive home behind gates on acreage, nothing like my parents' modest house, what we had by definition was an estate sale. My seasoned shoppers told me that an estate sale implies that a whole household is on sale, meaning more and better items. It is usually held indoors. A garage, moving, or yard sale implies that the person is cleaning house. These sales usually take place in the garage, driveway, or yard. A rummage sale invites people to dig for buried treasures in what some would consider the trash pile. Unwittingly, I managed to have all four at once.

TAKEAWAY

Value is relative. Make no assumptions about what has value and what does not. When you hold an estate or yard sale, you quickly learn the truth of the maxim, "One man's trash is another man's treasure."

7

How Much Is It Worth?

The Meaning of Value and the Fine Art of Appraising Antiques

"A thing is worth what it can do for you, not what you choose to pay for it."

—JOHN RUSKIN

"**N**ot for sale" read the lime-green sticky notes I had slapped on several pieces of furniture throughout the house. The notes blared out my ambivalence.

Not selling furniture was defeating my purpose, which I constantly tried to remind myself was *to clear out my parents' home to get it ready to sell*, not preserve what was left in it. The fact that I didn't live nearby was a mixed blessing. Otherwise I undoubtedly would have been tempted to cart more pieces home that wouldn't fit and would languish in my garage. The fact that anything I kept would have to be shipped cross-country added a layer of reason that kept my compulsion to cling in check—mostly.

But the task was defeating me. So much felt precious to me that I wanted to save it all. I felt the way I do when I go to the animal shelter: I want to take them all home.

"How much for the little nightstand?" the dealers inquired as they streamed through.

"I don't know . . . yet," I said lamely, pointing to the sticky note as some kind of proof.

Their deservedly nonplussed reactions conveyed the unspoken question, *Then why are you holding an estate sale, lady, if you don't know how much you're selling things for?*

Because letting go feels like hawking my fingers, I wanted to reply.

I didn't know how much the marble-lined nightstand that came from France was worth, or the gold-leaf chairs in the entryway, or the antique clock that was my grandfather's, or the cedar chest that was Grandma's.

Even if I did know, teasing sentimental value from market value is like separating beauty from a butterfly.

The experts would tell you—*have* told me—to take your time. Have someone from an auction house or consignment shop, a dealer, or an appraiser look at the items to determine their value before you sell.

That's great, but I did not have that kind of time. I had one week to get the job done.

What I did have, however, thanks to the panel of experts I'd amassed over the years of writing my home column, was an ace up my sleeve. I had connections to the folks at PBS's *Antiques Roadshow*. Gary Sullivan, one of the program's featured appraisers who specialize in high-end antiques, offered to let me run photos of my antiques by him to help me determine their value.

Using my 20/20 hindsight, if I had to do this over—and thank goodness I don't—I would have taken the photos sooner or had someone take them and send them to Gary before I got to the house rather than try to determine value while the two-day sale was in full swing. While I waited to hear from Gary, I fretted about losing cash buyers to my ambivalence and so cut some very uninformed deals based on my best guestimates and a dollop of prayer. As a result of being unsure of the value, I occasionally turned away interested cash buyers (though I took their names and numbers and told them I would call them when I had settled on an asking price) or made game-time decisions to sell stuff that I priced by using my best guess. (I'm not suggesting that approach but would completely understand if you ended up in the same boat.)

At every turn, I was torn between my twin goals of clearing the house so that the painters could start and being a good, respectful steward of my parents' belongings. Along the way, I did more waffling than a pancake house.

Toward the end of the first wild day of the estate sale, Gary called with his estimates of the value of the half a dozen or so items I wondered about. Before I share the particulars of what Gary said some of my parents' items were worth or weren't worth, here is some good general advice from him and others in the rarefied world of high-end antiques that will help you manage your expectations about the value of things.

WHAT'S IT WORTH?

Worth is a term Gary Sullivan would like to see struck from our vocabulary. "I'm forever hearing people say this is worth such and such and placing a value on an item far greater than what it would ever be sold for," he told me as I was grappling with placing a value on my parents' lifetime's worth of treasures.

"This is especially true of collectibles," he said. "I'm the bearer of bad news before I'm the bearer of good news."

Here's what Gary says we need to understand when trying to sell used goods:

- *It's just stuff.* The chances of anyone having something that has significantly great value are quite slim, Gary told me. Knowing this helped my lungs expand for the first time in three days. Unless someone in the family was quite wealthy and bought expensive things, a parent's home probably does not contain any great treasures. It's usually just stuff.
- *Age does not confer value.* Age—specifically being 100 years old or more—makes an item an antique. But to be a *valuable* antique, the item also has to be *rare and desirable.* My parents had antiques, but most were common. For those that were rare, the market wasn't that interested. That's the

desirability factor. That's reality. We'll look at some examples in the next chapter.

- *Worth is a worthless term.* The value a person states for a possession is most always far greater than what the item would ever sell for. That's especially true of collectibles. In a collectors' catalog—which often can be found online by searching by item type, such as Hummel collectible catalogs—an item will be listed for one value, but if you want to sell it, you won't get anywhere near that. Manage your expectations accordingly.

- *Sell wholesale.* Don't expect to sell an item for what you'd pay for it in a store. When you are selling household furnishings, set your price at the wholesale or auction value. Dealers have to resell the item for retail and in some cases have to fix it up. They have overhead and need to make a profit. Nondealers are expecting a huge bargain.

- *Condition matters.* If something is broken and repaired, it's almost as bad as if it were broken and not repaired. Collectors and dealers want merchandise that is in mint condition. Repairs are frowned upon. On furniture, the finish is important. Yet, sometimes dull and worn can be good. Collectors and dealers love patina, a sign of age.

- *Don't touch it!* During a lull in the estate sale, I started polishing an old brass lamp, but a dealer came in and stopped me. "Please don't," she pleaded. "The patina makes it appealing. A segment of consumers won't like it as much all bright and shiny." Gary confirmed that you should never polish, clean, or refinish antiques. If you alter some aspect of your item, such as its finish, you run the risk of greatly diminishing its value. Leave it alone.

- *Family history is usually wrong.* Remember the story of my friend's grandmother's "Tiffany" lamp? The legend of an item's provenance tends to grow over the generations. It's like the game of telephone. Everyone changes the meaning a little, embellishing along the way. An owner will say, "My great-great-great-great-grandmother brought this clock over from England on a boat in 1640." There may even be a letter inside saying so. But then you find that the clock was made in the United States in 1820.

- *Know your goal.* It's easy to get caught up in basing the prices of items on how much you would have to pay for them, but when I kept my goal in mind—clear the place out and exchange the stuff I don't want for cash—the prices fell. Our win-win motto was, "The more you buy, the less things cost," When a shopper asked how much for a lazy Susan filled with spices, I said, "Five dollars." "And how much without the spices?" she asked. "Eight dollars," I said.

YOU SOLD IT FOR WHAT?

Gary called at the close of day one of the sale. My stomach was in knots. Because I like to be in control of my own humiliation, I didn't immediately tell him that I no longer had some of the items he'd appraised. I waited until after his verdicts; I got out my pen.

As we talked, I chomped through a roll of Tums.

In addition to Gary's estimated value for these items, listed below, I will give you what I considered the sentimental value on a scale of 1 to 5, with 5 being the most dear.

THE OLD BLACK SETH THOMAS® MANTEL CLOCK hailed from Dad's side of the family. A sticker on the back dated it to 1883. The clock used to sound off every fifteen minutes. One day that stopped, and over the years we lost the winding key, or maybe someone buried it.   SENTIMENTAL VALUE: 2

SULLIVAN SAID: As an expert on antique clocks, Gary knows the Seth Thomas line well. In the late 1800s, the maker was churning them out by the bushel. "It's not worth much because, though it's old, it's just too common."

WHAT HAPPENED: I checked eBay and found dozens of similar clocks that had sold for between $56 and $150. Knowing that a clock shop would have to replace the key and clean the clock to get it running, I sold Uncle Ben to a boutique store owner for $60. "You sold for exactly the right price," Gary said. "In fact, you maybe got the better end of that deal."

AN ANCIENT-LOOKING SET OF TWO GOLD-LEAFED CANED CHAIRS AND A TABLE was among several pieces of furniture my parents brought to the United States from France, where they lived for a few years in the 1960s. The three pieces sat in our entrance hall, usually alongside the family dog. When a dealer offered $100 for the set, I excused myself and walked outside to cry. After a few minutes, I collected myself: What would I do with it? The pieces were rickety and would cost a fortune to ship to Florida, where they wouldn't fit in my home. I went back to the dealer who had made the original offer with a thicker skin and a stiffer lip and made a counteroffer of $200. SENTIMENTAL VALUE: 3.5

SULLIVAN SAID: The antique pieces were made in the late 1800s or early 1900s and were copies of period chairs from an earlier time. The fact that one of the seats was recaned (by Dad) diminished the value. The set would sell at an auction house for a couple of hundred dollars. An auction house would keep a percentage.

WHAT HAPPENED: I sold the set for $140. "That was a nice buy for the dealer," Gary said.

THE CEDAR CHEST once sat at the foot of my grandmother's bed, Dad told me. Grandma had nine children and somehow kept tabs on each one, including Dad, who was sixth in the lineup and probably needed watching. When he came home from a night out, he checked in with Grandma, and the two often talked while sitting on this chest. The chest maker's name, "Forest Park," was stamped inside the lid.   SENTIMENTAL VALUE: 4

SULLIVAN SAID: "These chests were a twentieth-century phenomenon. The company made them by the thousands. You're never going to find one that has any value as an antique. It's a $40 piece of furniture." I'd have "no regrets" selling it for near that price.

WHAT HAPPENED: I hadn't sold this piece yet. I weighed the low market value, the shipping costs, and the fact that I have three chests at home, and sold it the next day to a dealer for $50.

TWO HAND-CAST BRASS LAMPSHADES graced the living room for decades. They were beautiful and, my family believed, possibly valuable. Some dealers thought the lamps were antiques made from kerosene lamps. I had tagged them "Not for Sale" but took offers and phone numbers from interested shoppers.   SENTIMENTAL VALUE: 2

SULLIVAN SAID: "They are not early lamps." Before 1900, lamps didn't come in pairs. These were made as electric lamps in the 1920s to 1940s to look as if kerosene lamps had been turned into electric lamps. I told him I had an offer for $175 for the pair. He said to take it. "Their value is not based on antiquity."

WHAT HAPPENED: I called the buyer who had offered $175, but he flaked, a testament to the bird-in-hand maxim. I then called a dealer who had made the next highest offer and sold the pair for $150.

THE FRENCH SIDE TABLE, also from France, is perhaps the piece I'm fondest of not only because it was once my nightstand but also because I love its Frenchness. The piece has curved carved legs, a marble top, and a marble-lined cabinet (to hold the chamber pot, I was told . . . eww). It weighs a ton. I had no idea if the piece was worth $100 or $1,100. I did know that if I lived within driving distance, not 3,000 miles away, I'd take it straight home.   SENTIMENTAL VALUE: 5

SULLIVAN SAID: The piece was made in the late nineteenth or early twentieth century in the Louis XV style. The bit about the chamber pot isn't true. It was lined with marble to be a humidor for tobacco. The item would sell at auction for about $200. A retail store would sell it for $350 to $400.

WHAT HAPPENED: Despite buyer interest, I did not sell it at the estate sale. But after talking to Gary and forcing myself to be practical, I called one interested

dealer and offered it for $200 firm. He agreed, but the
morning he was to come get it, he changed his mind.
I think he expected me to lower the price, but I didn't.
After the sale, my parents' wonderful neighbors said
they would house the piece until I decided what to do
with it. It's still there.

THE DUNCAN PHYFE DINING TABLE had been the center of
every family dinner we ever had in this home, whether casual or fancy,
as the house didn't have a formal dining room. It was tough to let go of a
table that I had eaten at more times in my life than any other table and that
had been the center of hundreds of celebrations, holidays, and "every"
days. SENTIMENTAL VALUE: 4.5

SULLIVAN SAID: First off, Gary clarified, "It's a
Duncan Phyfe–*style* table." That's an important
distinction. (My parents had always referred to it as
a Duncan Phyfe, hence my confusion.) The table
and its four chairs were made in the manner of the
nineteenth-century Scottish-American cabinetmaker
but actually appeared to be midcentury saber-leg
Empire style cum Victorian. True, my parents bought
it shortly after they were married in 1948. "The value
will be largely based on how good it looks—if it has
a nice finish and color and will look good in a dining
room," he said. Beyond that, the table is "not rare or
important but strictly functional." If it's really beat

up, it will sell for $100 or less. In great shape, it would sell for $750 at an auction or more at a gallery.

WHAT HAPPENED: I turned down an offer for $150 and put it on Craigslist for $350. It wasn't ideal for a consignment because, I learned, many consignment store owners don't care for large items that take up a lot of floor space, which is something that resellers have to factor in to their overhead. After talking this over with Dad, whom we were calling with updates and who was intrigued by all this, we agreed to give the table to the neighbors' grown daughter, whom I used to babysit; she was now a young mother in need of a kitchen table for her home. That felt right.

THE CARVED PAIR OF DEMI TABLES together made a circle, but my parents split them so that each semicircular three-legged table sat on either side of the living room fireplace. The tables were carved and had black marble inset tops. They were pretty by my standards, and though I didn't feel particularly attached to them, I would have put them in my home. SENTIMENTAL VALUE: I

SULLIVAN SAID: "These are twentieth-century pieces of French provincial style, probably from around the 1940s. They're nice-looking but don't have a lot of value. They would sell in a consignment store for $200 to $300."

WHAT HAPPENED: I sold the pair for $150, which, Gary said, was "perfect."

LISTEN TO YOUR PARENTS' STORIES, THEN LET APPRAISERS SET THE STORY STRAIGHT

Because I was going through my parents' home like a woman with her hair on fire—the painters were coming!—I did not have time to have anything professionally appraised, with the exception of the advice Gary offered over the phone, which was both informative and comforting. However, I had had some home furnishings and art appraised before, and so I knew how it worked. If you have items you suspect are valuable, take the time to have them looked at by a professional. My appraisal story is typical:

The red lamps had been my parents' since before I was born. They had told me the story of those lamps, probably with some accuracy, but I likely had the story wrong. What kid listens to her parents when they prattle on about the origins of their home furnishings?

"And this porcelain figurine came from your great-aunt Myrtle, who came over on the boat back when the earth was cooling."

"Yada, yada, yada. Can I go to the mall now?"

When the man at the lamp-repair store told me I should have my red cloisonné lamps appraised because they could be collector's items, I tuned in. Collector's items? I don't collect anything unless you count shoes, age spots, bills, and items that depreciate faster than lottery tickets.

I tried to remember what my parents had said about them. Were these the lamps Mom bought at the Paris flea market in the

1960s? All I knew for sure was that throughout my young life, these lamps had stood on either side of my bed, looming like parents. I lobbied to get them out of my room in favor of something cooler, like twin lava lamps, but Mom insisted that they stay: "I like those lamps," she'd insist. She probably told me why.

When I moved out after college, the red lamps came with me because they were free. Now they flank my daughter's bed. She, too, has asked me to replace them with, among other suggestions, lava lamps.

"I like those lamps," I tell her, and actually mean it. When the lamps' sockets gave out, I took them to the repair shop. Then I took them to Kathleen Orozco, an accredited personal property appraiser, not because I planned to sell them but because if they were valuable, I'd make the kids take their pillow fights outside.

"Where did your parents get them?" she asked.

"Uhh . . . ," I stammered, then rolled out the Paris flea market story. To double-check, I called Mom, who, though then in her eighties, had a better memory than I did.

"No, no, no," she corrected. "The *living room* lamps came from the French flea market. The red lamps came from Japan. Here, let your father tell you."

She handed the phone off to Dad, who told me that while serving as a pilot in the Korean War, he visited a military base in Kobe, Japan. He bought the red cloisonné vases at a nearby souvenir shop and sent them to Mom, who was waiting for him back in California. She later turned them into lamps.

"I told you that story," she insisted, taking the phone back.

"You've told me a lot of things I should remember," I said.

"I won't comment."

I called Kathleen: "So they're not French antiques," I said, "but cheap foreign imports."

She applied her trade—a combination of historian, detective, curator, and therapist (for when people find out Grandma's Gorham® silver is really a no-name silver plate)—and the next day e-mailed her findings to me.

The impressive eight-page document detailed comparable vases sold at auctions and through antique dealers and provided a history of the period and process behind the lamp bases: Japanese cloisonné, circa 1900–1950, roses on a basse-taille ground of pigeon's blood–red enamel, manufactured, not handmade, and though of good quality, not rare. Replacement value: $600 for the pair.

Though the lamps aren't worth a lot as collectibles go, they're still special to me, especially now that I know the real story. Besides, who can put a price on sentimental value?

SHOWS ABOUT ANTIQUES SUCH AS *Cash in the Attic* (BBC/ HGTV) and *Antiques Roadshow* (PBS) have made many people look twice at their old stuff. "Just because you don't like it, that doesn't mean it isn't valuable," said Kathleen. The opposite is also true. But she taught me the following appraising lessons:

- *Use a pro.* Appraisers accredited by the American Society of Appraisers have had extensive course work in standards, methods, and ethics. Be sure your appraiser specializes in the sort of property you want appraised. Fees range from $100 to $200 an hour. A good appraiser is honest and won't appraise items outside his or her areas of expertise. For instance, when appraising an estate, Kathleen will appraise what she knows (furniture, silver, china) and then bring in experts in gemology, fine arts, and antique rugs as needed.
- *Figure out what kind of appraisals you need.* Insurance appraisals yield the highest values because they state an item's retail replacement cost. Fair market appraisals are for sales between willing buyers and willing sellers or for cases involving divorce or charitable donations. Marketable cash value may help those who want to liquidate quickly.
- *Value is relative.* Intrinsic quality, condition, fashion, the market, age, and scarcity all determine an item's value, which can fluctuate.
- *Know what and when to appraise.* Appraise items you think may be valuable so that you

can itemize them on your home insurance,
with photos and documentation. Older
people often appraise their valuable furniture
for estate-planning purposes, said Kathleen,
"so their kids don't set the Chippendale
chairs out in the garage sale."

- *Go online.* A faster and often better way to
  get information is by researching it yourself
  online to find the value of common objects.
  You often can get a good sense of an item's
  market value from eBay. Check the sold
  price, not the asking price.

- *Leave things alone.* Change the function
  and you devalue the piece, said Kathleen,
  repeating a lesson others have shared.
  "Don't turn a Biedermeier dresser into a sink
  vanity."

- *Listen to your parents' stories.* Stick notes
  behind artwork or in drawers of good
  furniture that state when, where, and why an
  item was purchased and for how much. Even
  if the item isn't valuable, some day the story
  may be priceless.

TAKEAWAY

Obviously, most things aren't worth the cost or time to have them appraised. If you don't want to pay for a full appraisal and don't need to find out an item's provenance but want a good idea of whether it has significant value, Gary suggests contacting an auctioneer, consignment shop, or dealer in your area. "A true expert should know when an item isn't worth appraising," he said, "as well as when it warrants closer inspection." For common items, frankly, the information on eBay, and to a lesser extent Craigslist, because it tends to reflect local markets and deals with many noncollectors and noncollectibles, is the most valid representation of real-time market value. They are amazing resources and have changed the world of reselling used furniture, antiques, and collectibles.

8

For Art's Sake

Art, for What It's Worth

"I had rather see the portrait of a dog that I know, than all the allegorical paintings they can show me in the world."

—SAMUEL JOHNSON

Perhaps no other category of household goods is as difficult to put a price on as art. Appraising fine—or sometimes not so fine—art is an art in itself, so much so that you may need an appraiser who specializes in that area.

Whether it is a painting on a wall, a sculpture, or a handmade quilt, some art can sell for head-scratchingly high prices. Thus, I was stumped by how to price my parents' artwork, almost none of which—except for a couple of oil paintings—I wanted for my home.

As I looked at their art, I tried to conjure the stories they shared over the years about where they got a certain oil painting of waves breaking or one of a shady, tree-lined lane on a fall day. (In the case of the latter painting, they told me the woman artist who painted it had been married to a famous painter, who, my mother was sure, had had a hand in this canvas. She mused that this made it worth more.)

I didn't know if any of the artists were important, but I sure didn't want to find out after I'd sold something for $10 that it was a sought-after original that later sold at an auction for $100,000.

Ultimately, I was able to make a relatively good stab at pricing the artwork to sell, thanks, once again, to my multitalented friend Aaron LaPedis, who had taught me a few things about art appreciation one afternoon years earlier in my home in Colorado.

We met Aaron in Chapter 2 (see pages 14–17). Well, he also owns an art gallery in Denver: Fascination St. Fine Art.

Besides knowing how much the stuff in your garage is worth, he knows art. To get a crash course in how to size up art and its market value, I invited Aaron to my Denver home to look over my art and show me how he assesses various works.

Before then, I had little idea what my art was worth, let alone the art in my parents' home. Like them, I bought the art I have because I liked it. Sometimes I've purchased a piece to fill a space or because it worked with my home's design and color scheme. I wasn't trying to make an investment. My collection, and I use that term loosely, was a mix of inexpensive oils by knockoff artists who copy and churn out pieces by the dozen and art my kids made in grade school. I also owned—by sheer fluke—art worth more than I paid and works from artists whose paintings now hang in museums.

I HAD INVITED AARON OVER because I wanted to learn how a pro could tell the good stuff from the pedestrian. I wanted to see a pro size up art and find out why some art that looks great can be practically worthless whereas other works that look baffling to many people wind up on a museum wall.

Aaron came over and confirmed what I suspected: "The most talented artists aren't necessarily the ones who make the most money," he said. "And great art doesn't always make a great investment." There are a number of high-profile commercial artists who aren't necessarily the best artists, but they have really talented marketing people behind them, he explained. Everyone knows who they are, and that's worth something.

As Aaron surveyed my art, he paused before a large, three-by-four-foot oil painting in my office and said, "This looks valuable. Tell me if it is."

I shook my head. "One hundred eighty dollars framed," I said.

Aaron eventually would have uncovered the piece's real value when he turned it over and saw that it was painted on poor-grade canvas and learned that I had no certificate of authenticity. But I was flattered that it passed his initial scrutiny.

Then he looked at three oil pastels I had bought twenty years earlier, when I was a struggling writer in graduate school in Vermont and wanted to support a struggling local artist whose work I admired.

IT'S NOT A FUNERAL: JUDGMENTS AND FALSE PLATITUDES

After day one of the two-day estate sale, I collapsed in bed on the verge of a coma. The fact that the coma did not come was an ambiguous blessing, because in its place furniture dreams tormented me. In them, I saw rooms of my parents' old furniture, with dealers laughing (*mwahaha*) and rubbing their hands greedily as my parents said, aghast, "You sold that for what?"

All that day and ultimately the next, when faced with selling my parents' antiques, finer furniture, and everyday stuff, I felt caught in the crosshairs, frozen at the intersection of clearing the house in a few days so that we could fix it up to sell and honoring the value of their treasured belongings.

The next morning, the house was again buzzing with buyers who knew a lot more about what we were doing than I did.

But this time I noticed a false sentiment that was beginning to grate.

"I'm sorry for your loss," a buyer said as he streamed through the front door, barely making eye contact.

"Thank you," I said, mirroring his somber note but wondering to myself: Loss? What loss?

"My condolences," said another buyer a few minutes later.

What? This was an estate sale, not a funeral.

"Thank you," I said, feeling once again like the last person to know what was going on.

The third time a stranger expressed heartfelt remorse, I got it: *They think my parents died*. I wanted to say, "Oh, we're just downsizing, moving my parents into a smaller place with more support," but that felt like too much information, besides being none of their business.

Most estate sales apparently happen postmortem.

To the next buyer who expressed condolences, I tried to clarify. "Oh, thank you," I said, "but my parents are still alive. They've just moved on."

The stranger looked at me weirdly, as if I were some spiritual kook. "I mean on to assisted living," I added too late. She didn't hear me, but another one did and shook her head disapprovingly, as if selling my parents' stuff while they were alive was tacky, though that didn't stop her from shopping.

It's not like you think! I wanted to say, then stifled myself and thought for the ten-thousandth time that life is complicated.

Even when you're doing your level best, people judge you, and not always accurately. I needed a third skin, to endure. I wanted to explain to these people that my elderly parents moved out because a fully loaded four-bedroom house became too much for them, that I was selling the contents and eventually the house—*with their permission*—to help pay for what I hoped would be many more years of their retired life. I also wanted to tell them the story behind every item in the house and what it meant to me and my parents, but that was too much information to download on someone who was pretending to care but really just wanted to know whether I'd sell the bookcase.

Let's be honest: These polite phonies didn't know my family and surely didn't care about my attachment to the stuff that was my parents', and to be blunt, most of them probably didn't really care if my folks were dead or alive. I must balance this by saying I also met some truly first-class collectors and dealers who raised the caliber of the sale significantly just by being there.

"I'M SORRY FOR YOUR LOSS," said another buyer, removing his hat respectfully.

"My parents aren't dead!" I said, perhaps too firmly.

"Boy, am I glad to hear that!" another shopper said. "Because I won't buy anything that belongs to someone who died."

I must have screwed up my face, because she added, "Bad energy."

I nodded as if I understood but thought she was a pint short of a quart.

I share all this because I thought it was weird, though probably common, but mostly because I needed to get it off my chest.

___

"I like what she does with color," he said, "but her work is too complicated to make it in a popular market." He was right. Though her work now hangs in the Museum of Fine Arts in Boston, she's not well known, just talented.

Here again, the Internet is your best friend. Isolate the name of the artist who created the piece you want to sell and do a search, Aaron advises.

- *Representation.* First you want to know who the artist is in the art world and if any galleries represent him or her. The more galleries that represent the artist, the better. If only one or two do, the chances of that artist's being well known are low, and so are the chances of reselling his or her work. Also find out if the artist's works have been published in books. An artist whose works are valuable often has one or more books published on his or her work.
- *Museums and awards.* Try to find out if the artist's work is in any museums and whether the artist has won any prestigious awards. I had one plein air–style oil painting by a Laguna Beach, California, artist who went on to win the Collector's Choice Award for the Laguna Beach Plein Air Painting Invitational, among others. Aaron said that probably would double the value of his work.
- *Limited edition.* If a painting is so popular that a market exists for limited-edition prints of it, the original is probably valuable.
- *How original?* There are degrees of originality, said Aaron. Some pieces are 100 percent original—they were created

by the artist directly. Others are signed and numbered limited-edition prints: lithographs, serigraphs, or giclées. Others are "artist marked," in which case the artist retouched a print with his or her own hand. Although not 100 percent original, they are worth more than an unretouched print. I have one like this.

- *Size matters.* When sizing up the painting, consider its size. "When appraising art, size matters," said Aaron. "Given two original pieces by the same artist, the bigger one will be worth more."

- *Find the papers.* It also helps your cause immensely if you have a certificate of authenticity. Ideally, keep it in an envelope tucked behind the piece so that the certificate and the art don't get separated. "If the originality of the work is ever challenged, you will lose if you don't have this," Aaron said. An older work of art may have documentation concerning the sale of the piece over the years: who and where and when it was created and when it changed hands. This is known as the *provenance*.

At the home front, Aaron's lesson served me well.

TAKEAWAY

Art needs to be appreciated on two levels: how much you like it and what it's worth on the market. There can be a great distance between these two assessments. Art that you love and that works beautifully in your home or has sentimental value because it was your grandmother's may not be worth anything on the market but could be invaluable to you. Conversely, some art that would fetch a high price may not find a place in your heart or your home. Keep both of these measures in mind when determining what to keep and what to let go of.

9

Beyond the Estate Sale

What to Sell Where

"Take only memories, leave nothing but footprints."

—CHIEF SEATTLE

Remarkably, in just five days—three days of sorting, organizing, and pricing and then another two days of a selling frenzy that would make Black Friday look tame—we turned half the household contents into more than $3,000 in cash.

However, the feeling of relief that so much was gone was short-lived. Once I saw how much was still left—household items that did not sell (or that I would not sell) and my "pile of postponement"—I realized that much work still lay ahead.

That was when I turned to my other liquidating options. When Aaron LaPedis gave me the ground rules for having an estate sale or garage sale, he also gave me golden advice on what to sell where.

An estate sale is an excellent way to clear out a house, but it's not the only option. In fact, the best way to liquidate a household is to use a combination of methods.

GARAGE OR YARD SALES

For a home you still live in but want to thin out (that sound is me clapping), have a garage or yard sale. These sales are great for getting rid of household stuff worth less than $100, said Aaron: garden tools, baby furniture, kitchenware, clothes, and any item you would never take the time to put on Craigslist or other local classified sites. The best part of having a garage sale or yard sale is that it's free and you get the money right away.

INSIDE TIP: **Accept only cash.**

CRAIGSLIST

Like an online yard sale, Craigslist and other local classified sites are perfect if you want fast cash and don't want to pay someone else to sell your stuff. It's the right venue for larger, lower-end, but still usable items such as bedroom sets, office furniture, and appliances. Because buyers are local (or should be), you avoid shipping costs, which can exceed the value of an item. To list a piece of furniture, you need to create an online account and post a few pictures along with an honest description, including the item's measurements. Interested buyers will e-mail or call you (give out a cell phone number instead of a traceable landline) with questions. The process usually moves well-priced items very quickly.

After the estate sale, we sold half a dozen items on Craigslist, including the guest bedroom set, two sofas, a large desk, and some bookshelves. The site is a great way to sell big items that could still benefit someone, just not you.

INSIDE TIP: Sell only to buyers who will pick up the items. Again, accept only cash. Do not accept checks, certified checks, or wired money. When a buyer is going to meet you, meet for the first time in a public place, bring your cell phone, and have someone with you. Try to avoid inviting strangers into your home and if it is a small enough item, make the exchange in public. If it is a very high-value item, Craigslist suggests making the exchange at your local police station.

EBAY

Although Craigslist is perfect for large items and local buyers, on eBay the world is your market. On this online auction site, you will want to sell smaller, more valuable items such as collectibles and fine jewelry, which are easy to ship. Here you also will have to set up an account. The pictures are really important. Take the time to polish the jewelry and light it well, then photograph items with a good digital camera in high resolution from several angles. Include a close-up of the label, mark, or stamp if the item has one. Because you will open up your buying pool to a world of buyers, you probably will get a higher price than if you sell it on Craigslist or through an estate sale. You also can set a reserve—a price under which you will not sell—and a "buy it now" price so that bidders can take the item off the table. But before you count your earnings, don't forget to factor in the cut you will give to eBay and PayPal. Expect to pay eBay up to 13 percent of the sale price and possibly a small listing fee. PayPal, which provides a secure way to pay, takes another 3 percent. If you decide not to charge for shipping as an incentive, you have to add it to the other charges and might see 20 percent taken out of your gross sales.

INSIDE TIP: Use PayPal to handle the money. It's the safest payment method as it protects both buyers and sellers. Never send anything without requiring a signature. Aaron also recommends insuring shipments.

VENDORS

Another way to unload your items is to sell them to a reseller, such as a flea market, antique shop, or secondhand store. But because resellers need to make a profit and also have store overhead, be prepared for them to pay you only about 25 percent of the value, which, believe me, can be worth it.

INSIDE TIP: Consider this option as being one step above dona-tion. The exception is if you can take a tax deduction for your donation, and save more in taxes than you would get in a vendor sale. You need to do the math.

CONSIGNMENT

Local consignment stores can be a godsend. You take your gently used furniture to them. They sell it and split it 30 for you/70 for them or sometimes 40/60. Bear in mind that most consignment shops do not want to devote their often tight spaces to large pieces unless the items are in good condition and desirable to the current buying market. These stores are often great for smaller items such as artwork and lamps.

INSIDE TIP: Most consignment stores will keep dropping the price at regular intervals until a piece moves. Be sure to read the contract so that you're aware of the timing and amount of these markdowns; that way you won't be startled when you get less than you bargained for. Some stores also include in their contract that if you don't pick up the piece after a period of time, it becomes their property.

JEWELRY BUYERS

Despite what you (or your sweetheart or relative) paid, expect to sell gold and silver jewelry for the meltdown value. I know. That hurts. The exceptions are fine watches and jewelry from high-end designers. (Think Tiffany®, Van Cleef & Arpels®, and Cartier®.) Jewelry stores or gold buyers will buy your gold for its weight and purity. Go to a few buyers and compare offers. "Never put your gold in a bag and ship it to one of those outfits online and wait for a check," said Aaron. "You will be at their mercy."

If you plan to sell gold—and I have done this several times—watch the market (go to www.goldprice.org). Gold fluctuates, and you can often do better if you wait even a few days. All gold buyers base their offers on the current market price. Take your gold to several buyers and see if they all come up with the same weight, which will be in pennyweights. Also see if they agree on the grade of the gold, whether it's 14, 18, or 24 karat. For example, I once had a chunky 14-karat gold bracelet that was very masculine and dated; I had offers between $995 and $1,500. As I was not going to wear it, I considered the rather unattractive piece as unused money sitting in my drawer and took the best offer. I also had one gold buyer tell me a solid 14-karat gold necklace I had wasn't all gold, only gold-plated, despite the stamp. He tried to buy it for $50. (Be careful out there.)

If you have a piece of gold jewelry with stones in it, you probably won't get anything for the stones unless they are precious, such as diamonds or emeralds, or large and rare.

INSIDE TIP: Don't walk into a gold buyer's shop with a bag of gold without having first watched the market rates for a few days to make sure you're selling when prices are on an uptick. Then get more than one offer to compare.

COLLECTORS

Rare books and collectible coins do sell on eBay, but sellers may do better going through an auction house that specializes in selling items made in multiples that are collected in sets. Big-time collectors may scan eBay but feel more confident buying at auctions, where a professional has reviewed the item. Here are some of America's top auction houses for antiques and collectibles: Bonhams, Christie's, Freeman's, Heritage, Hutter, Sotheby's, Skinner, and Swann.

INSIDE TIP: Take some time to find out where the serious buyers go to find what you're selling and follow them.

AUCTIONS

Consider taking truly high-end antiques (my parents' home, as we learned, didn't contain any pieces that qualified), along with any fine art, to a local antiques dealer who can take them to an auction. If your item is worth more than $5,000, contact Sotheby's or Christie's in New York about selling items at one of their auctions, advised Gary Sullivan.

INSIDE TIP: Auction houses typically take 10 to 15 percent, but so does eBay. Find out what the house's take is up front as well as where it will place the starting bid.

PAWN SHOPS

Go only as a desperate measure. Pawn shops typically offer only 10 cents or less on the dollar, Aaron said, and so I avoided them.

TAKEAWAY

Before you stick household goods you'd like to sell out on the driveway, first be sure you're not missing a better selling venue. For instance, more valuable furnishings and artwork often fetch a lot more at antique and art auctions.

10

The Treasure Hunt

Tackling the Pile of Postponement

> *"There comes a time in every rightly-constructed boy's life when he has a raging desire to go somewhere and dig for hidden treasure."*
>
> —MARK TWAIN

The first cut is not really the deepest one after all. The last one is.

After a rough and ruthless week of letting go of a lifetime's worth of home furnishings in the estate sale and on Craigslist, I still faced the pile—no, let's call it a pyramid—of postponement, a mound far bigger than it should have been, which contained family photos, letters, military memorabilia, and other artifacts of my parents' long, fruitful, well-lived lives.

In my effort to clear the house for the painters, I had pushed these items into the old home's garage, saying: "I'll deal with you later."

I now better understand how seemingly pulled-together people turn into "someday" people who fill basements and garages or, worse, storage units with their parents' old things, close the door on it all, and tell themselves that "someday" they'll deal with it.

Here I was, after five days of taking apart the house a piece at a time, sorting and selling—Mom's costume jewelry, Dad's tools—and I finally understood what all these buyers offering me condolences were talking about. Letting go item by item feels like a hundred small deaths.

It's the end of an era.

Finally I understood the buyers who had left me so perplexed by their frequent expressions of sympathy: "I'm sorry for your loss."

Now I was saying to myself, "Me, too."

Condolences were in order.

Ushering off items that I had known all my life, which were inextricably tied to my parents and thus to me, and sending them out the door with perfect strangers should have felt like progress, but it felt like organ donation.

Although I could in that moment have fallen into a well of self-pity deeper than the Black Hole of Calcutta, I shook off the nostalgia.

I had only a few more days in town, and I needed to tackle my next task, which was to sort through the remains: what buyers didn't buy and what I wouldn't sell—in other words, my pile of postponement.

Filling half the garage and part of the driveway were items ready for the Salvation Army truck, which I had scheduled for a pickup the next day. That would make a dent, but the tough stuff would still be there.

Meanwhile, I also needed to make a dozen decisions about necessary home improvements to get the house on the market, including what color to paint the walls, which the painters thought might be helpful. I wanted to say, "Do I look like fifty women to you?" But it wasn't their fault. First things first.

I surveyed the remains. Moving them all into the garage gave me a false sense of organization and calm. The fact was that I was still facing total chaos. Now it was just corralled chaos.

As I looked at everything—in addition to the photos, letters, and military documents were dozens of slide carousels, paintings we couldn't part with, and other family treasures like the wooden cigar box Dad got from his dad—I tried to figure out how to draw the line between what to let go of and what to keep. I needed to find that sweet spot on the continuum between nothing and everything. I thought about everything I had ever written about clutter and the mounds of advice from the experts I have grilled.

I mentioned in Chapter 4 that procrastination is the root of all clutter. I was finding that ambivalence is procrastination's evil twin.

Save? Donate? I didn't know.

Throughout the clearing process, the words of declutter king Peter Walsh were my mantra: "When everything is important, nothing is important."

Peter is right, of course. As much as you might want to keep everything that touches you, if you kept everything that meant something, it all would mean nothing. And you really would have too much stuff.

His advice brought to mind my college economics class. In the one day I stayed awake (do not schedule economics classes right after lunch), I managed to learn about the law of diminishing returns. It's paradoxical but true: The more you have of something, the less you appreciate it. The more heirlooms you hold on to, the less meaningful they are.

When you begin to separate the memory from the material, you can begin to let go.

Therefore, as I faced the pyramid, I called Peter, whose next piece of advice truly did become my guiding light.

GO ON A TREASURE HUNT

"Imagine," Peter suggested, "that your parents have deliberately left you five treasures. Your job is to find the items that have the strongest, happiest memories for you. Go through not in sadness but in loving memory. So look with joy for the few, best items to keep. Let the rest go."

Then, he said, display them with honor and respect in your home so that every time you walk past them, your heart sings.

"I don't want to trivialize this," he added, "but if someone loved you and nurtured you and brought you into the world and into adulthood, that person would never want you to suffer or be in anguish or despair over his or her possessions. You have to believe that your parents, wherever they are, would be looking at you and saying, 'Come on. I don't want you agonizing over a china set or a wedding dress!'"

I combined that thought with our sorting guidelines from Chapter 2. Those guidelines are easier to apply—I am not saying *easy*—when you are trimming the excess from a house in which you still live. The guidelines are exponentially harder to apply when you add the thick emotional factor that the belongings are your parents', that you are now responsible for the family history, and that the cuts must be much deeper because you have your own fully loaded home.

But as Mom always told me when facing tough times: "The best way out is through."

Into the pile I went, keeping these edicts in mind:

- *Need, use, love.* Remember these words. Together they constitute the acid test. Do you need it to live your life right now? Would you use it? Do you love how it looks? If you answer yes to any of those questions, it may be a keeper.
- *Add your own filtering questions.* This is not a one-size-fits-all exercise, but these additional questions served me well: Does it mean a lot to me, and why? Will it go beautifully in my home? Is it worth shipping? Do I have a place for it? Am I keeping it out of guilt? Will it burden my kids?

- *Choose meaning over value.* "Don't grab the most valuable pieces," said Gary Sullivan, who for years did estate liquidation sales for families. "That's what people do, but that's not the right decision. Keep what means something. If you have an antique that a dealer is willing to buy for $5,000 and you decide to keep it, you just bought it for $5,000. Ask yourself if you would pay that, because you just did." Take the belongings that were special and that give you the greatest positive connection. "If you love your mom's dinner dishes and could use them, keep them," Gary said.

- *Choose small over large.* I loved some of my parents' larger furniture items, but the shipping costs were prohibitive. I get just as much resonance and connection from the pearl necklace Dad bought Mom. These pieces are far easier to pack, ship, and store. "Don't underestimate the cost of housing and maintaining an item," said Mark Brunetz.

- *Get your story straight.* Ask what the story is that *you* attach to the item, not the story with which your parents endowed it. "The minute an item transfers from your parents' house to yours, it's no longer about the meaning they endowed it with," Mark said. "Once you're clear on your story, you can cut what you decide to keep in half. That becomes a touchstone for determining what to keep."

- *Remember the present.* Letting go helps you live better now.
- *Check your sentiment.* How you love someone lives in your heart, not in an inanimate object.

Although the tendency is often to keep more than is wise, Gary finds the opposite to be just as sad.

"Over the years, I have cleaned out countless estates, deciding what to auction, consign, and donate. I'd sort through everything, and it often struck me, once I saw the lifetime of belongings of now-gone family elders spread out, how the next generation could leave and close the door like it never existed. It's nice when there is family involved to take some pieces, keep them and cherish them, and carry on the memory."

That said, he added, "The things my parents cherished don't mean much to me and mean nothing to my kids. The formal dinner sets they got as wedding presents, which were once very expensive, they're not sought after today. Focus and interests change. For the most part, prices come down. It's a generational thing; you have to stay in step as times change."

True, my parents' style wasn't mine. Nonetheless, as I went through the process, I was tempted to keep too

PIANO LESSONS: LETTING GO OF THE STORY

"Stories like 'but it was expensive' or 'it has sentimental value' or 'I can give it to my kids someday' are what make us hang on to stuff we don't use or need," Mark told me. "Those stories trap us. Let go of the story and you can let go of the stuff weighing you down."

"Why does it feel like a chunk leaving my soul?"

He said something else I glommed onto: "The world is full of useful items, but if you don't use them, they're not useful to you."

For instance, I once had a piano in my family that had a story. This was in my adult home, when I'd become a parent, so it is not my parents' story. The story goes like this:

Once upon a time, there were two little girls in Colorado who took music lessons—one the piano, the other the flute. They were my daughters, full of hope and promise. And I got caught up in a dream of a home filled with music and children discovering hidden talents thanks to parents who would gratefully sell their right arm if it meant securing their kids' futures.

Well, the piano player's interest soon hit a decrescendo, though the $110-a-month payments for the cherry upright in our living room endured. And endured.

By the time it was paid off, the piano's bench hadn't creaked open in a year, and the only music in the house was piped out of iPods.

My kids grew up, and we eventually moved out of the Colorado house, but the piano stayed in the living room of the home, which another family moved into and rented. Only this family had their own piano dreams and their own piano, a baby grand. And they wanted my upright out.

Not so easy since we were now living in Florida. Thus, yet another item had gone from aspiration to albatross.

I listed the piano on Craigslist in Denver, a market flooded with dead piano dreams. I spread the word around my old neighborhood and told my daughter's former piano teacher and anyone who might be interested to just make an offer.

The piano teacher mentioned it to the grandmother of one of her young students. The grandmother bought it from me for her granddaughter, a little girl adopted from China who already was playing virtuoso pieces. At home, all she had to play on was an electric keyboard; now she would have a real piano.

I sold the barely played piano for a fourth of what I paid for it.

So the piano will fill a home with music. Just not my home. And it will fill a dream. Just not my dream. And you know what? That's really okay. Because it wasn't useful to me, but it is to them. And that's how it should be.

---

much. But I continued to winnow the "keep" pile, remembering Peter—"When everything is important, nothing is important"—and my assignment: the treasure hunt, the hypothetical last task parents leave their children.

"If your mom and dad could see you, they'd kick you in

the backside and say get on with your life," he said. "They want you to be happy. They don't want to drag you down with their stuff."

With that notion steeling my spine, I selected my treasures. Trying to keep keepsakes to a minimum, I tucked a few pieces of Mom's jewelry, including her pearl necklace, into my carry-on and shipped three boxes to my home. In them were an oil painting of French hens, a mainstay in our old kitchen; three handkerchiefs monogrammed with my mom's initial (one for each of my daughters and one for me); a set of gold-edged stemware because it's beautiful and I will use it; and several other items. The total was a little more than five, but Peter's guiding light helped me stay well under the fifty items I might have brought home if I hadn't applied some restraint. Later I would have my parents' china and silver shipped to my home.

Weeks afterward, I reported to Peter what I had brought home. "I can tell by the words you used—'I love it. She loved it. I will use it.'—that you chose exactly right," he said. "Consciously or otherwise, you found the treasures."

I let out a sigh so huge that I levitated.

But I had to confess, "At first, when I saw the chicken painting in my kitchen, my heart did not sing. It broke a little. But now, and this has taken weeks, I love seeing it every morning."

"That's the test," said Peter. "Welcome to adulthood."

When I look at these items in my home now, when I

wear Mom's pearls, or when I pull the gold-rimmed glasses out to set the table, my heart does sing. And that's the proof.

> **TAKEAWAY**
>
> "Make it a treasure hunt. Imagine that your parents have deliberately left you five treasures. Your job is to find the items that have the strongest, happiest memories for you. So look not in sadness but in joy for the few, best items to keep. Let the rest go."   —Peter Walsh

11

The Really Tough Stuff

What to Do with Photos, Wedding Dresses, Military Medals, and More

"Some memories are realities, and are better than anything that can ever happen to one again."

—WILLA CATHER

Now, don't get the wrong idea. I didn't just vanquish the pile of postponement with one big personal pep talk. I had dozens of mental wrestling matches with myself, such as the one I had over the crocodile purse (see page 97). But given what we'd started with, 98 percent of the belongings were sold, saved, donated or dumped, and we had cleared $4,800 for our parents.

But I still wasn't done. I had made many grueling decisions and let go of pieces as if they were body parts, and now I faced the über-tough stuff, items that brought me to a full stop.

These were among the most emotionally charged belongings, the kinds of cherished pieces that many people have to deal with. I consulted my "cabinet" once again and my own ravaged heart and came to the following conclusions. Your decisions may differ, as these choices are different for everyone, but on the following pages I respectfully offer you some ways to consider how to honor these items.

MOM'S WEDDING DRESS

I found the wedding dress wrapped in blue paper and tucked in an old suitcase, the way Mom had kept it after she and Dad were married in August 1948. The dress had been made by hand by an Italian seamstress for $35.

"A wedding dress like that is such a beautiful, wonderful, emblematic thing," said Peter Walsh. "Hold on to it. Maybe one day it can be worn, or made into a christening garment for a grandchild, or used to wrap bouquets in a daughter's wedding."

Mark Brunetz, however, sees it differently and offered this wedding dress advice: "Your mother's wedding dress is clearly emblematic of a special day and an important love relationship, but it was *her* special day. It has served its purpose. If no one is going to wear it again, have some nice pillows made out of it."

For now, I have the dress, still in its suitcase, and know I will find an occasion to use or reuse it. However, I also came across this great idea for other garments laden with memories: Maybe it's a dress your mother wore on her fiftieth wedding anniversary, a joyful day. Clip a piece of fabric from the anniversary dress and put it in a frame with a photo of your parents and keep that, rather than the whole dress, in your home.

LOVE LETTERS

My dad was a sweetheart. We have letters to prove it, pages and pages he wrote to Mom over the course of their courtship and marriage. What do I do with them? "I'm going to get emotional telling you this," said Peter, "because I've done it. First, remember, the letters are not really yours. They are part of a romance between your parents and were never meant for you." Peter, who has six siblings, gathered with family members on his parents' anniversary. They shared their letters, told stories about them, and at midnight, burned the letters. "We ritualized them and sent the love back into the universe."

FAMILY PHOTOS

My Dad was also a slide man. I have so many boxes containing carousels that if they were stacked, the pile would tower over me. "Photos have particular power and importance that make it feel like sacrilege if you throw them away," Peter said.

No kidding. Sorting through the photos—and I didn't get through all of them—was one of the most emotionally difficult and labor-intensive tasks I faced in this whole process. Going through them is like looking at a flip book of life passing quickly by. Nothing feels sadder.

Pull out the great ones and send them to an online service, he advised. Let the rest go.

I have done this for my family photos at ScanMyPhotos

(www.scanmyphotos.com), one of many scanning services. Others use Snapfish and make albums or coffee-table books.

The goal of photos is to preserve memories, but no one wants to look through all the unedited photos of a lifetime. "If you edit them well, your family can easily look back, and isn't that the goal?" asked Peter.

My dad actually helped me with this one. When I asked him what I should do with all his slides, he said, "Throw away all the ones of landscapes. Then pick three with people in them from each vacation or holiday."

Then Peter handed me this bit of tough love: "To say you want to hold on to them all is an adolescent response. When you can accept the passage of time, even when that means accepting the death of a parent, that's what it means to be an adult."

MILITARY MEDALS

My parents met during World War II on Okinawa. Dad was a marine fighter pilot, and Mom was an army nurse. Their medals are framed and with them in the assisted-living center where they live. When that chapter of their life closes, my brother, Craig, has claimed them for his home, which is as it should be.

For Peter, his father's medals are sacred. "As we speak, I'm standing next to my dad's framed medals," he said. "They remind me of his bravery and how he built a family. That is the treasure my dad left me. That is all I need."

THE CROCODILE PURSE: HOW TO WEIGH SENTIMENTAL VALUE

It's different for everyone, the one item that detonates a firecracker string of feelings that seemingly has no end. For me, it was my mother's crocodile purse.

When I was a girl, I loved going through my mother's pretty things. She had a mirrored tray of perfumes, which I'd open and inhale. She had a drawer full of jewelry, with stories about how each piece came to be hers; a scarf drawer that smelled powdery and luxurious; and a shelf full of purses.

Most of the purses—or pocketbooks, as she called them—she used, but one was tucked inside a red velvet drawstring bag like a bottle of rare brandy.

The brown crocodile purse within was, of course, the one I endowed with the most glamorous appeal.

It was a sturdily structured handbag, the opposite of today's feed-sack style, with a well-proportioned strap handle. A tidy gold clasp held it firmly closed. I never saw her carry it.

But I imagined a day—before her life was overtaken by full-time work as a school nurse, two rambunctious kids, church activities, and warp-speed domesticity—when she might have.

I wanted to believe that once upon a time she had a dashing younger life, and the crocodile purse fueled that picture. I imagined that the purse in the velvet bag was reserved for fancy occasions.

However, Mom's life wasn't fancy. The only time I saw her dolled up was once a year for Dad's office holiday party, which she admitted she didn't enjoy that much. Mostly my parents were content to stay home or socialize with church friends, a ho-hum, non-crocodile-purse bunch.

But there had been one big night. In Sens, France. My father was transferred there when I was an infant, and we stayed a few years. One evening my parents dined at a restaurant in a posh hotel. It must have been a special occasion, an anniversary, perhaps, because she talked about that dinner for years.

The butter came curled, she said. And they had escargot.

Fast-forward five decades. Mom is in an assisted-living center, and I'm cleaning out her purses and trying to sell them in the house that was once her home, my parents' home, my home. I was trying to make quick decisions about what possessions to keep, toss, or sell, but I hit a hard stop when I came across the red velvet bag.

I slid the crocodile purse out reverently. I looked inside and saw a folded paper, brittle and yellow with age: the menu from the night she dined at the hotel in Sens. This was indeed a big night in her life; she'd carried her best pocketbook.

This is what happens when you clear out a loved one's home. You're plowing through a closet and wham! Maybe it's not a crocodile purse with a folded menu. Maybe it's a college diploma or military uniform or a high school yearbook from the 1940s that forces the question: What do I do with this now?

I looked at the purse and applied the acid test: Do I love it, do I need it, will I use it?

I took a dispassionate look at this romanticized object and saw it for what it was: an old woman's handbag, too passé to be fashionable. The handle was cracked with age, not use. I couldn't picture myself ever using it, nor either of my daughters. But still, it had sentimental value.

I paused to think about why Mom had saved a purse she never used for all these years. And an answer came: because it reminded her of another time, another side of her that she hung on to so that she could show me who she once was.

As I looked at the purse and the relic of a menu, I realized in that moment she had just done that. That was all the purse needed to do.

Later, I told my daughters about the crocodile purse, and we talked about Grandma's big night. I painted a picture in their minds of their grandma as a dashing young woman out on the town with her handsome husband. And we let the purse go.

TAKEAWAY

Marriage and birth certificates and college diplomas are important family records. As my parents' executor, my brother, Craig, has these documents in a file. But he has also scanned them, along with their will, and so I have a copy. For me, and maybe for you, a scanned memory—or in this case a record, as I wasn't there when they were born or married—is enough.

PART TWO

You Don't Have to Do This Alone

ENDOW: To give or bequeath; to provide with a quality, ability, or asset. From the Old French *endouer*, "equivalent to"; and from the Latin *dōtāre*, "to dower."

12

What the Pros Know

Behind the Scenes at an Estate Sale

"The ordinary acts we practice every day at home are of more importance to the soul than their simplicity might suggest."

—THOMAS MOORE

Just because I chose the full-immersion experience of wading through my parents' possessions one at a time doesn't mean that's the only way to do it or even the best way.

It was just my way.

Although some families know that selling their parents' furniture is neither a job they want nor one they can bear, which is perfectly rational, I felt differently.

Plus, my parents, and by extension me, have always been frugal. I didn't want to take a cut of the profits, which were going straight into their long-term-care fund.

In my heart, I believed that was what would honor and please my parents the most, though they surely did not want to leave me a burden.

Anyway, looking back—which is another way of saying wising up—I see the value of what I did and have a new appreciation for the value of experts.

For starters, professionals know how emotional, irrational, and deluded those of us selling our parents' belongings—heck, even our own stuff—can be when estimating value: *But those were our baby bibs. They're priceless!*

A growing number of companies specialize in helping folks of all ages and at all stages downsize and liquidate estates. I'm going to introduce you to several; they all get the job done, though differently.

In this chapter, we'll go behind the scenes at a professionally held estate sale where family members were decidedly not present. In the next chapters, we'll meet a trio of siblings who worked together to clear out their family home after their mother—and last surviving parent—died, using the services of an online auction company. We'll speak to Barbara W., who needed to downsize when she moved into her daughter's home and couldn't take it all with her. We'll meet two couples that both took a proactive and admirable approach to downsizing before their kids had to deal with it.

We'll also meet business owners who work alongside older adults and families to help them downsize sensibly and sensitively while finding good homes or sales venues for what they can't take with them.

THOUGH NOTHING CAN PREPARE YOU for the shock of sorting out your own family home, several years before I faced the task, I experienced an estate sale from the inside. For a column I was planning to write, I tagged along with

Dewey Smith, a fine furniture appraiser who also conducts estate sales for higher-end estates.

Of course, even though I did not know Lucy, whose home we were liquidating, I couldn't help feeling sad. This is what life comes to. I could see how much she loved nice things, and she had them.

But at age ninety-six, Lucy didn't feel like keeping up her home anymore—which I totally get—and so she moved into an assisted-living residence and hired Dewey to sell the stuff her kids didn't want.

I arrived before the doors were open, and there was already a long line outside. I excused my way through and was let in, which seemed to ruffle the crowd.

Curious, I began looking around at how things were priced. Being in a stranger's home flipping over price tags should fall somewhere between tacky and illegal, but Dewey, who gets 20 to 30 percent of the sales, assured me it was all business.

Then he said in a warning tone, "Get ready." He nodded to the crowd outside. He and his helpers assumed their posts. At 10 a.m. sharp the door opened, and bargain hunters covered the place like ants on a honey puddle. The next few hours felt like rush hour as adrenaline-fueled shoppers stripped the place of furniture, old rugs, artwork, dishes, and books.

"And I thought I knew how to shop," I said to one helper.

"Some get paid to shop," she said. "They're pickers who shop for dealers who don't have time."

"I'm in the wrong line of work."

I watched buyers home in on their specialties. One couple made a beeline for a French antique upright chest so heavily carved that an onlooker could have gotten lost in its crevices. Dewey said he already had a buyer for the circa 1880 chest, priced at $5,800. An A-list dealer at the presale had made an offer, which Dewey would accept if no one topped it.

Presale? A-list? Dewey explained: At high-end estate sales, there are A-list buyers, who are dealers and collectors with money. They come to the private sale. The B-list includes dealers and collectors with less money. They get invited to the presale. The C-list is everyone else.

Because Dewey is so good at organizing sales, every customer thinks he or she is on the A-list. "You have to be careful. It's easy to insult people," he said.

INSIDE TIP: "It's unethical for the person representing your items for sale or appraising them to also buy them." —Dewey Smith

Before this sale, Dewey already had sold Lucy's grand piano (for $20,000 or so) and some fine artwork.

An Iranian man and his blond wife zeroed in on a $900 Lavar Kerman rug. Where I saw a worn-out rug that I'd apologize for, they saw value. The man explained that the nine-by twelve-foot wool rug came from Lavar, an Iranian town, making the eighty-year-old item rare. He and Dewey settled on $600; the man then anxiously rolled up the rug so that shoppers wouldn't wear it down more, as if after eight decades, one more hour would matter. The couple sells old rugs online. They'll get $2,000 for this one as is, the wife estimated.

Though I was learning every minute, I hadn't learned what I'd hoped to after hanging out for a day with Dewey at an estate sale: how to spot a valuable piece amid a bunch of junk. "That takes a trained eye," said Dewey. And, I suppose, as with the finely aged rug, time. But I did learn that there are people out there, dealers and collectors, who have a black belt in shopping.

Here's what they know that the rest of us don't:

- *What's not hot.* "It's hard to tell little old ladies what their figurines aren't worth," Dewey said. Silver plates, collectors' plates, and china are also not big sellers today. Not long ago, sets of antique fine china from classic brands commanded nice prices. But today's consumers want fine tableware that's dishwasher and microwave safe. An eighty-three-piece set of traditional fine china at this sale went for $400 (less than $5 per piece).
- *Deal breaker.* Pet contamination hurts values. No matter how much you love your cat, claw marks, accidents, and residual odors mean rugs will need cleaning and repair and upholstered furniture will need re-covering. Dewey pointed to a moth-eaten spot in an

old wool rug priced at $1,200. The price would have been higher, but the cat had done its business there. Moths had feasted on the protein to lay their eggs, and . . . ugh. I got the picture.

- *Internet effect.* As more retail stores close in favor of selling online, small items are becoming hotter. They're easier to store, pack, and ship. Thus, large furniture pieces often languish; that means buyers expect deep discounts, and sellers need to price accordingly.

- *Get the words right.* When describing an object to sell online, learn the lingo by reading other entries. For instance, quality and condition are not the same: Something of good quality can be in lousy condition. Be very specific and accurate.

TAKEAWAY

If you have a chance to shop at a professionally organized estate sale before you try to downsize your own family home, I strongly recommend that you go. Being behind the scenes at this sale years before I had to do the same thing for my parents helped prepare me mentally and emotionally.

13

The Siblings

The Year of the House

"Brothers and sisters are as close as hands and feet."

—VIETNAMESE PROVERB

Up there in the category with death and taxes is this inevitability: At some point almost everyone will have to clear out a parent's home. That's how Peter Brenton of Boston, who with his two older sisters cleared out their childhood home, looked at it.

Their mom had died the previous year, and they were in the process of slowly and painstakingly going through the household.

"It falls into the 'most stressful' category," said Peter, with whom I felt an instant rapport, having just gone through the same process.

"It's like having open-heart surgery without anesthesia," I said. He agreed.

Their father had died ten years earlier, Peter said. Their parents had been married for forty-five years. After her husband died, Peter's mom left the house just the way it was until she died.

"Our parents weren't classic hoarders," said Peter, who was forty-seven when we spoke and one of the most clear-headed people I had ever talked to. (When I learned that he worked as an administrator in a university engineering department, it made perfect sense.) "But they hung on to a lot of things they saw no reason to throw away."

"Tell me about it!" I said. I thought of the dozens of gift bags Mom had stashed and all the vases from every floral arrangement she'd ever received.

"Financial papers and receipts that went back thirty years," he said. "Wedding gifts they received in 1955, which they didn't like and never opened. Guns and ammunition."

"Wait. Guns and ammunition?"

"I don't have a gun license," he said. "In Massachusetts it's illegal for me to carry even a bullet. What was I supposed to do with this?"

"The memorabilia was excruciating," said his oldest sister, Anne. "Mother was so sentimental and saved so much over the years. We would open box after box marked 'miscellaneous photos.' They would have black-and-white photos of people I hadn't thought about in fifty years, along with birth announcements and receipts from the cleaners. Every box was like a time capsule."

"My parents had the exact same boxes!" I said. "You open one and fall into the deepest dark well."

"They had the classic stuff that accumulates unless you get rid of it," Anne said.

Because every family moves through the process differently, some better than others, I was curious to hear how the Brenton siblings managed.

Their mother had died in February 2012, about eighteen months before Peter, Anne, and I chatted. That spring, they began to tackle the house. The three siblings met at the homestead every Sunday to chip away at the possessions. They took the summer off and picked up the routine again in the fall, spending a total of five months of Sundays, Peter estimated, going through the belongings.

They pressed forward because, as their brother reminded them, the house was costing them $1,800 a month to carry.

"As the executor, Peter felt the weight of the job," said Anne, who was fifty-five at the time. "He was the practical one and kept pushing. My sister and I would have let things sit for a year."

"As executor, I was probably a good choice because I place less emphasis on the value of stuff," said Peter. "Sometimes I had to be more firm than was polite."

Making matters more difficult, he said, was the fact that he and his sisters were all historically inclined, yet none of them had a huge house. "Our homes were already full of our own objects that had sentimental value. Although there were things we all felt were precious, none of us had room."

They didn't like the thought of just storing stuff in their attics. "Why store something you're not going to enjoy?" Peter reasoned.

They didn't need to explain that to me. I wanted to cling like a barnacle to every remnant of the lives that were slipping from me, but I also did not want to add to my own load.

The first two Sundays, they filled two industrial-size trash containers. That was the easy part. "Here's where it got sensitive," Peter said. "Most Sundays we worked six to seven hours; some days we would spend much less time. We would have a big fight and would have to leave. These were stupid fights. We didn't fight over anything in particular."

The day they spent sticking their names on items they wanted "ended in a horrible argument," he said. "None of us was blameless."

"I love my siblings," Anne said, "but we had to pull away."

"We fought not over any one thing but because of the emotional weight of sorting through it all," Peter added. "We all had this huge burden."

"Every time you get together and meet siblings at your old house," Anne said, "it knocks you over like a tidal wave. It was fun and painful. We each wanted to sort through it in our own way. We had some arguments."

Most siblings assume that everyone sees the items and the process in the same way, but that rarely happens. Siblings need to recognize that each of them comes to the process with a different agenda based on their value systems, Susan Gardner, a professional organizer and founder of Clearing the Way Home (an older-adult move management company), told me. This was truly eye-opening, as I thought everyone approached the process pretty much the same way.

But that is not so. One person may be very sentimental and approach the process entirely based on the sentimental value of items, she said. Another sees dollar signs and looks at how much money can be gotten from the sale of the goods. A really practical sibling will focus on getting the job done and strategize on what has to be done to get from full house to empty house. Another may take a more circular path and go room by room with no concrete plan.

Knowing this—and I now see that Susan is right—helps explain the tension otherwise cordial siblings encounter.

In my family for instance, my brother, an architect, is a minimalist. Although he doesn't lack love and respect for our parents, he doesn't gravitate to their stuff. His response when I asked if he wanted anything was, "No; it was theirs, and it has served a useful life." He really wanted very little. His wife, Chickie, who loves to bake, wanted only Mom's shortbread pans.

I clung to a few more items, but still not much. We had no instances of rivalry over wanting an item. If anything, we were saying, "You take it." "No, you take it."

The Breton siblings, by contrast, had items that more than one of them wanted. Therefore, they made a rule: Nothing would leave the house without all three agreeing.

"There were the Christmas tree decorations we grew up with," said Peter. "The green glassware that was my great-grandmother's. The tabletop statue of a moose that our dad bought in Germany in 1953 when he was stationed in Stuttgart. Every object had a story."

How well I knew.

"What I wished was that my mother was sitting there with me going through this stuff," said Anne. "I wished she had been willing to go through it when she was alive. But she wasn't up to it."

ANNE KEPT THE silver, their baby cups and spoons, some engraved items, an antique desk made by their great-grandfather, and a few small pieces of furniture that would work in her home. But she knew to exercise restraint: "I'm at an age where I would like to be selling and downsizing and would like less to take care of," she said.

"I looked for things that I remembered the story from," said Peter, "or remembered my parents really valuing but also that I had room for and would use." One item is a monogrammed key box his father carried in his pocket so that the keys wouldn't poke holes in his pockets. It was small, personal, and useful.

When two antique clocks became a little contentious because Peter wanted both and so did his sisters, this realization helped. "I really didn't want both clocks," he conceded. "What I really wanted was to keep them in the family. It wasn't important that they were in my house."

One now graces his entry.

Whenever the siblings lost focus or their spirits lagged, Peter reminded his sisters of the goal: to empty the house and eliminate the carrying costs. It would serve them all to clear it and sell it. In the end, they stayed focused: "We were very goal oriented in getting the house empty," he said.

GETTING OUTSIDE HELP

But from the get-go the Brenton siblings knew they would not be able to go through an estate sale. "We simply wouldn't be able to face that," Peter said.

In October, seven months after their mom had died, all the personal items had been sorted and tossed or saved. But apart from what the siblings took for themselves, the bigger items remained. They brought in an outside company their realtor recommended that specialized in liquidating households quickly.

Such businesses are becoming more popular as the age wave in this country is putting thousands of older adults each day in the situation of clearing out either a parent's home or their own.

Among those serving several states are companies such as Everything But The House and MaxSold. (Others do this work, too. Those people looking to clear out a home can get local assistance by calling an auctioneer in their area, which they can find by contacting the National Auctioneers Association [www.auctioneers.org]. Some, not all, will liquidate households.)

MaxSold is a Canadian company that is in over twenty states in the United States, including Massachusetts, where the Brenton family home was. The company (www.max-sold.com) sends in a team that organizes household items in batches or lots, photographs them, and then uses social media to sell them locally through online auctions. The company's founders have fifty years of combined auction experience.

"The falling value of many goods alongside the rising cost of shipping and delivery has created a great market for the local auction," said MaxSold cofounder Barry Gordon. "We combine the wonders of social media with years of auction experience to liquidate households swiftly."

Another growing company is Everything But The House, a similar service based in Cincinnati that offers an online auction to buyers worldwide. The company did nearly $11 million in sales in 2014 and is currently growing by more than 150 percent per year, said company president Andy Nielsen. As of 2015, the company had grown to serve sellers in twelve states and fourteen markets. While such companies can help sellers net more profit than they might if they hosted a traditional estate sale, they also give families a reality check about what their stuff is worth on today's market.

"Like many people, we thought there was more money in stuff than there really was," said Peter. "The things that our parents' generation thought valuable are not valuable to the current generation. We weren't out to get the highest price, but the company helped us see that their pricing was appropriate for the goal."

In two weeks, MaxSold grouped, photographed, cataloged, and auctioned off everything (more on their process in Chapter 14).

"It was a dramatic clean sweep," Peter recalled. "For people in our situation, who were paying the costs of holding on to the house, this was absolutely worth it."

Whereas Peter chose not to be present the day buyers picked up their purchases, his sister made a point of it. "I felt so much better after meeting and talking to the buyers, telling them the history of my parents' treasures," Anne said. "We all have our own way of getting through."

Yes, there were moments of regret. For instance, she watched a baby grand piano go for $120. "If I had known, I might have tried to sell it privately, but it was a relief to have someone take it who would appreciate it."

When she catches herself in that downward spiral of thoughts about items that were auctioned off that she wishes she still had or wishes she had tried to sell for more, Anne summons the voice of her mother. "Mom would have said, 'You have to let that go, honey. It's gone. You have what's important: your memories, your children, your life. You have to live your life.'"

In October, MaxSold, through an online auction, liquidated every last item in the home, down to the mops and buckets. In November, the Brenton siblings put the house on the market. The sale closed in January 2013, eleven months after their mom died.

"It was the longest year of my life," said Anne. "You see the world through a different lens."

> **TAKEAWAY**
>
> Some families need to sort and sell their family belongings themselves, but others benefit from hiring an objective outsider. Consider the culture of your family and then decide.

14

What's a Household Worth?

Putting a Price on the Priceless

"For where your treasure is, there will your heart be also."

—MATTHEW 6:21

It's true. Some things in life you just can't put a price on.

And then you have to. When it's up to you to liquidate your parents' treasure-filled home, you need to price the priceless.

How much for the sideboard that served up every Thanksgiving dinner you can remember? How much for the porch swing Dad built?

When selling is both unthinkable and necessary, outside experts can be a godsend.

Not that I would know. While I was able to call on experts, I basically had myself, my sister-in-law, one week, and a learning curve that didn't curve at all but shot straight up like a flagpole.

MaxSold cofounder Barry Gordon put it bluntly: "Things are worth what people will pay. The buying market will determine the value, not the seller."

He helps sellers get the right mind-set by asking them, "Is your goal to get top dollar or to clear the house?" If the goal is to clear the house, getting too hung up on what something is worth is not only a distraction, it also works against your goal.

"We are a conversion service, an auction vehicle that turns household contents into cash," he said. "It's not for us to say what any item is worth, but we introduce our view."

One of those views is this: "There's a saying in business, 'The first offer is the best offer.' Those who insist that this item is worth a set amount and won't sell it for a penny less get stuck with it."

He sees firsthand how dealing with a family home can paralyze loved ones. "It can take the toughest, most organized, efficient people and slow them to an absolute standstill," said Barry.

Yup.

"Our process is not designed to replace the important work," Barry explained, referring to the sifting, sorting, and saving that family members must do first. "But once the family decides what won't stay, they need to get out of the way."

They need to hire experts to sell items or be realistic about the pricing. If nothing else, the process of going through stuff from the past is a reminder that life is short. "We don't need to work ourselves into a frenzy trying to control things we can't," Barry said. "You can't control what others will pay you. You can control how much of your life you put into the process."

That process, he said, takes about two weeks from start to finish. In the first week, the team sorts and batches items into lots. A lot might contain one item, such as a piece of art, a nice lamp, or a sideboard; it can be a collection of ceramics; or it can even be the contents of the utility room, including the mop, broom, bucket, and rag basket. Selling items in batches helps sellers clear a large number of items efficiently.

Bundling items is a tactic I wish I'd done more strategically. Although I had put like items for the estate sale together—Mom's two dozen dried flower arrangements, her forty-some flowerpots—I had tagged each item individually rather than saying "$30 for all florals." You'll move more merchandise faster and more efficiently if you make groups: all figurines, all items in the cleaning closet, all pots and pans. "Buyers can't pick and choose," Barry said. "They buy the whole lot."

The team then photographs the lots and creates an event catalog.

The next week, the auction starts. "We go hyperlocal in markets, because 99 percent of what people sell, they sell in their neighborhoods," Barry said. And they market through a variety of social media avenues.

When the auction concludes, credit card payments are collected. After payment is secured, buyers have two days to pick up their lots. Most auctioneers then collect a percentage of the total sales or a set fee and return the balance to the family. MaxSold, for instance, collects 30 percent of the total sale or $1,000, whichever is greater. The rest goes to the family.

Meanwhile, sellers have to abide by certain rules. One is no reserves. (A reserve bid in auction is a price below which a seller will not sell.) "We don't allow that," said Barry. "We ask sellers, 'Are you done with these items and are you prepared to release them to the competitive market?' If they are, we sell."

It's a trap to think that setting your price or having a reserve ensures that you will get the price you want, he said. "Only place a reserve if you're prepared to keep the item. If the goal is downsizing, reserves may leave you dealing with tougher choices about how to sell or otherwise dispose of the item or pay storage fees."

I know. I turned down several offers for my parents' antique marble-topped nightstand, which, as I mentioned, I still have parked at a family friend's house across the country.

Clinging has its costs, especially if you need to ship an item, move it, or, heaven forbid, put it in paid storage. (Dear readers, please, before you get a storage locker, call me. I will talk you off the ledge.)

Barry cites this example: Say someone has a dining-room set and would feel awful if it sold for anything less than $2,000. A buyer offers $800, which the seller turns down. Then, because there's no room for it, the set goes in storage. Three years later, at $100 a month, the seller has paid $3,600 to hang on to it and finally sells it for $500.

Better to yank the bandage off now, even if it hurts. And it will.

WHEN MOM MOVES IN

When Barbara Weinz moved from her Maine home into the Massachusetts home of her daughter and son-in-law a year ago, she knew she would need to downsize. But the eighty-one-year-old antiques dealer owned not only a houseful of precious items but also a store full.

At first she moved almost everything from her store to her daughter's home, thinking she would set up an antiques business in her new town. When that didn't pan out, she stored the antiques and collectibles in her daughter's basement.

"I was cluttering up their basement," she said. "They weren't complaining, but I got the message."

She also recognized that if something happened to her, she would be leaving quite a burden for her two daughters and their families. "I wanted to lessen the burden on them," said Barbara. "If something happened to me at my age, what were they going to do? They would have all these items they would know nothing about."

She, too, contacted MaxSold.

"I was pushy with them about how they marketed the items," she said. She wanted to be sure the pieces' pedigree and provenance were featured properly. "They were very good and very cooperative."

It took less than three months for her to unpack, sort, and work with MaxSold to get rid of it all, which she considered fast. The team put together seventy-five lots, and all of them sold.

"I did fairly well, better than I expected," she said, "considering the situation and the market for antiques."

ALTHOUGH NO TWO HOUSEHOLDS ARE ALIKE, in Barry's experience, the contents of the average North American home, after the family members have taken out what they want to keep and paid the liquidator 30 percent, nets between $3,000 and $10,000. He's heard other liquidation professionals say the average house yields about $5,900. That may be tough to swallow, but it is realistic.

As for my parents' home, after the estate sale, which brought in about $3,000, we continued to sell items on Craigslist, in consignment stores, and to dealers. Ultimately, we cleared a total of just under $5,000. But we hadn't yet sold the biggest asset of all, the home itself. That was next.

How long the job of clearing a house takes also varies widely and is highly individual. "I've seen clients go through the process in light speed, burning through the sorting in a day, and others take several years and still do not make much progress," said Barry. "A good healthy time frame is probably a couple of weeks."

A SOLUTION FOR SIBLING RIVALRY

Those who work in the business of liquidating family estates have seen it all, from families that turn the process into a big grab fest and fight over who's getting more to remarkably gracious families.

Susan Gardner, of Clearing the Way Home, said, "Because we know family members approach the situation differently—some are sentimental, some are value driven, some highly task oriented, and some process oriented—you need to come up with systems that respect and acknowledge each style."

For the Brenton siblings, as we saw in Chapter 13, that meant everyone had to agree on who got what before any items left the house.

When Gardner and her four siblings were sorting their parents' belongings, she said, they put a number on every item in the house. Then each sibling wrote down the numbers belonging to the items he or she really wanted.

"When a number came up, if two or more people wanted it, they drew straws," she said. "If one person was getting too lucky, we would adjust. There was a graciousness among us."

Another system some families use entails putting a monetary value on every item. Each sibling is allotted an equal budget to "shop."

The point is to even it out, said Susan, and have a system.

MaxSold's Barry Gordon prefers not to get in the middle.

"We're not family counselors," he said. "We're a liquidation service." When a parent leaves an adult child an estate that has economic value, the parents don't want to confer a problem. "They want to confer their assets and their wealth. They don't want their kids to spend years fighting with each other and being stressed."

But for siblings who want the same item, he has one surefire way of handling the situation.

If three family members want the same item, he handles it this way: The item goes to auction, and the siblings bid on it along with the public. That establishes market value. If one sibling makes the high bid for, say, $600, he or she gets the item.

But to settle up with the other two siblings, they treat the money as if the item had gone to an outside party for $600. If that were the case, each of the siblings would have gotten $200, assuming the profits were to be divided among them evenly. But with Barry's method, the winning sibling gets $200 subtracted from his or her portion of the profit, and the other two siblings each get $200 for the "sale" of the item plus an additional $100 each (the high bidder's share is divided between them).

In this way, the auction provides a pathway for the family to deal with disputes fairly.

Investing in relationships while loved ones are alive is far more rewarding than fighting about their stuff afterward. In the end, those conversations will stay with you longer than the crystal candy bowl.

FACTORING IN SOME ALTRUISM

After a career helping older adults transition to assisted living, David Stennes, of Minneapolis, came up with his dream charity: Harvest (www.harvesthelps.org).

"I kept hearing the same question from my clients: 'What do we do with all this stuff?'" said David, who e-mailed me after coming across my series of newspaper columns on clearing out my parents' home. In the e-mail, he asked, "If you had known we were there to take the valuables, store, photograph, and catalog them, have them valued and sold, with the revenue shared, would you have done that?"

I called him up and asked him about his business model.

"I looked at the numbers and saw that we're at the beginning of a huge age wave," David said, noting that every day 8,000 Americans turn sixty-five and that this will continue until 2030. He then explained his altruistic model.

"My premise is simple," David said. "If the network to pair the lifetime accumulation of household goods with other families in need exists, is it worth considering?"

Harvest helps those who are clearing houses find homes for their household goods and furniture in a way that benefits the lives of others. His team clears everything from a family home, separates what can be sold from what can be donated, and sells the nicer items online. The nicer items are sold one of two ways: either online at Etsy or Furnishly.com or by consignment to a network of local dealers and designers, he said.

Items he can't sell he donates to charities, including thrift stores, churches, and homeless women's shelters.

He looks to recover the costs he incurs by selling a household's better furnishings. After covering his costs, he returns the profits to client families.

BULK BUYERS

Some folks who need to clean out a home fast call in a bulk buyer. This is considered the most desperate measure and, believe me, it's tempting. A bulk buyer will clear all the contents of a home and dispose of them as it sees fit.

They operate using different models. Some charge you to haul the stuff away. Some charge nothing and hope they can sell some of the belongings to cover costs and make a profit. Others come and look at your home and make you an offer for the whole lot. Although this might be the perfect option for someone with little time or patience, for a family that knows the contents of the home are pretty much worthless, or for someone who physically or geographically can't manage the project, be careful of hiring a service like this when you're in a vulnerable spot. To me, some of these services can seem a little predatory.

However, if that's a route you want to try, you can find a bulk buyer in your area by searching online under "Complete household buyers" plus the name of your city. Good luck!

If there aren't enough nice items to cover Harvest's costs, David charges a small fee to offset its costs. Though their service is currently available only in the Minneapolis area, he hopes the idea catches on. He'd like to franchise the concept beyond Minneapolis. "I want to replace the sting of letting go with the knowledge that it all went to a good home," he said. He hopes that spirit will change the future of estate sales, downsizing, and clearing out family homes.

"Not only could it be psychologically valuable to have help from others while working through the nostalgia," David said, "but also the help will save adult children time away from work and family, and the energy required, which is physical and emotional."

TAKEAWAY

When clearing out a home, many families, including mine, hold an estate sale in which individual items are tagged and the public is invited on a particular day. The sale can (and did for me) create a chaotic environment that is hard to control, especially if a lot of people show up. Others work with a bulk buyer, who pays one price to take everything away. What you lose in profit you gain in convenience. A liquidator, such as the auctioneer services mentioned earlier, is a hybrid. It batches and auctions off goods from the house and reports all sales to the client. The growing field of senior move managers offers a variety of tailored and very personalized services to older adults looking to downsize.

PART THREE

Downsizing Up

DOWNSIZE: To reduce in number or size; to make smaller; to simplify (one's life, for instance), as by reducing the number of one's possessions.

15

Moving On

How to Know When It's Time

"We leave behind a bit of ourselves
Wherever we have been."

—EDMOND HARAUCOURT

Not to get too philosophical about this, but you come into this world with nothing and leave with nothing. In the middle is the bell curve called life, which is front-loaded with a time for acquiring and growing. Typically, you, or you and your partner, get your own place with your own stuff; maybe you get married and buy a house. If you add kids, your planetary footprint expands. This feels like progress, and it is.

It's wonderful, and fun, and exhilarating, and filled with added responsibility.

When we reach the top of the curve and start down the other side, it's natural, or should be, to wind down gradually. Kids leave the nest and start their own lives, and the household gets smaller, or it should. That's all natural.

For years I was part of the move-up movement. Each

time I moved, my home got a little bigger, a little grander, and that felt, in a uniquely American way, like progress.

A growing young family and a (usually) promising housing market whisked those moves along in the way a strong ocean tide pulls a swimmer down the shore.

But though I still love a big ole gallivanting house with a big yard, that's not a fit for me anymore. It is for a growing family, but on my side of the bell curve, such a home doesn't call to me the way it used to.

Although many choose to stay and grow old in the family home, as my parents did, others don't have that option. (By the way, not choosing to move, and instead preserving the status quo, is also a choice.)

Circumstances led me to make a different choice from the one my parents had made. Though not an easy decision, my move taught me, among other lessons, to reevaluate what I wanted and needed—not in a house but in a home, and I mean *home* in every sense of the word. It also taught me a lot about downsizing.

In 2011, my oldest child was heading off to college. My youngest was finishing her sophomore year in a high school she didn't like. I was approaching the half-century mark and realizing that my twenty-plus-year marriage could not be sustained. Also, after years of freelance writing and not working full-time, I realized I had some abilities I wasn't using. I felt as if I were riding a ten-speed bike but only using four gears. I wanted to get back in the game, use all my gears, and reboot my career.

I was offered a newspaper job as a senior reporter in Florida. Knowing that my younger daughter was eager to move and go to a new school, I accepted the job, and my daughter and I moved from Denver to Orlando.

We left a very large house that my husband and I had built and had put a lot of love, sweat, and money into, and where I had lived for eight years and raised children and had at one time seen as my forever house.

As much as I wanted to avoid the discomfort and the unknowns of moving to what would surely be a smaller, less grand house, when I was honest with myself, I knew I had to. My home, as beautiful and full of good memories as it was, was holding me back.

"But Mom," I remember my oldest daughter saying to me, "you've put your heart and soul in this house. How can you leave it?"

I hope she remembers what I said: "Darling, no house is worth hanging on to if it doesn't support you anymore."

The Colorado house was rented to a young family with four children, who filled it up nicely. Then I fell into an interesting housing opportunity: I became a live-in home stager, moving into higher-end homes for sale and staging them with my furniture until they sold.

Apart from the obvious drawbacks—chronic tidiness and frequent moves—this arrangement had two very big advantages: First, I got to live in nice houses for about 40 percent less than what they would cost to rent. In light of what I was accustomed to and what sort of housing I would be able to afford on a journalist's salary, this made for a soft landing. Second, and more important, it gave me flexibility. Because I wasn't sure how I would like my job, or if it would like me, or if my daughter would like her school, I wanted to avoid a long-term lease and another mortgage. This setup gave me flexibility.

Since I left Colorado in 2011, I have lived in and staged six homes in four years. When I left my large three-story Colorado house, I sold nearly half the furniture to the new tenants, who would have purchased more if I hadn't needed some furniture in Florida to stage my digs. (I tell you all this to let you know that I "get" downsizing.) I took about 30 percent of the household with me; my husband took the rest.

Lost in the transition, and not on purpose, were two decades of Christmas decorations, a casualty I profess to be grateful for but that I honestly still can barely talk about without a stiff drink.

My downsize and relocation happened the year before my parents moved into assisted living, but the conversations leading up to their imminent move were under way. So, in a way, my parents and I were living parallel lives, each breaking from homes that had been the epicenter of our lives.

I knew that leaving my Colorado home would be hard, but looking ahead at my parents' move from a home they had lived in for literally as long as I could remember, I knew that when that happened, their world would stop turning on its axis. What I didn't appreciate at the time—but would later learn—is that my world would stop turning on its axis as well.

All this was on my mind when I was asked by the unsuspecting editor of a lovely shelter magazine, *Mountain Living,* if I, being a sort-of-known voice in the design world and of late a Rocky Mountain resident, would share my design resolutions for 2012.

In previous years, I would have prattled on about my plans to remodel more frugally or more sustainably or experiment with painting furniture or bolder wall colors, but my mood was different. Though the editor probably was expecting a response along the lines I just described, my answer was more reflective. You see, I literally was remodeling the concept of "home."

"For me," I wrote, "it's a time of transition. So I'm looking at all I own and all I may acquire in a new way and asking, Is it nimble? So my family could evolve, I sold a lot of furniture and kept only those items that would kill me to part with and that would look good in many spaces. If a piece isn't versatile, handsome, well made, and nimble, I'm not interested."

HOW TO KNOW WHEN IT'S TIME TO MOVE

No, it wasn't easy to leave a once-full rambunctious home where I'd thought the days of raising children and keeping up would never end. (The years are short, but the days are long, a wise woman once told me about the child-rearing years.)

I can look back and say that as scary as that cross-country move was, it was the right one. It allowed me to reboot my career, reshape my life and priorities, and send my daughter to a better high school.

Moving—whether up, out, down, or on—is never easy, said life-change expert Russell Friedman, coauthor of four books, including *Moving On*.

"Even when you're moving for positive reasons—a better job, a better house, better schools—moving is a major grief event," said Friedman, who is executive director of the Grief Recovery Institute in Sherman Oaks, California.

He defines grief as "the conflicting emotions caused by the end of or change in a familiar pattern of behavior."

I could be his poster child, I told him during one long conversation.

What I came to understand in this journey is this: A home—and I don't mean a house—must be elastic. It must give, expand, and contract while helping you hold it all together, like a good pair of control tops.

And when it no longer does that, it may need to go.

Let me repeat that: *When your home no longer fits, it may need to go.*

PROCESSING GRIEF

Back at the assisted-living center, Mom—as is common for anyone but especially for those experiencing cognitive impairment—was having trouble with the change.

"I feel like a misplaced person," she repeated like a mynah bird when I called or visited her in her and Dad's new apartment. Dad just shook his head. He was bearing the brunt of the guilt for a decision that had been hard to make but necessary. Mom kept saying she wanted to go home. The confusing part was that she was home.

I knew the feeling.

The notion of home—both the home of my childhood and the primary home for my children—was shifting, making me realize that home, along with the concept of it, is so very relative.

"This is just temporary," Mom said for the tenth time in an hour. "We're going home tomorrow. I feel like a misplaced person."

"I know just how you feel," I said.

"But this is just temporary," she said.

"Yes," I said, thinking that everything is.

"We're going home tomorrow."

"That's true," I said. She would be right here.

The sadness should not be minimized but felt, said Russell Friedman, the grief expert. "Ignore anyone who says you can replace the loss," he said. "Rubbish. Loved ones, pets, houses, friends are not replaceable. They're relationships, not lightbulbs. Accept the change and the grief that comes with it."

That is part of being alive and being human.

ALTHOUGH MY COMPULSION TO NEST is stronger than any bird's, I know at the cellular level that a home's job is to support those who live there, not enslave them. When where you live weighs you down like a boulder, it's time to roll that stone.

Russell heartily agrees: "Many people don't make changes at home they need to make because they're afraid of the feelings they will have. They're fearful, so they stay stuck in an unrewarding place."

"Oh, I am on a first-name basis with fear, postponement, and uncertainty," I told him.

"You have to take some action and trust that the parachute will open. There's got to be some faith in the leap," he said.

"I'm also personal friends with the great unknown," I added.

Change, he said, is hard because our brains crave the familiar and want things to stay the way they have been.

The longer you've lived somewhere, the harder it is to move, said Paula Davis-Laack, an attorney turned resilience expert and blogger for *Psychology Today*. "Our brains often work against us, providing lots of evidence for, and reason why, it makes sense for us to stay."

The rationalizations, avoidance, and desire to preserve the status quo keep us root bound. Though I'm not recommending my steady diet of upheaval, I am suggesting that those who are feeling stuck and housebound and yet are contemplating a move to downsize should find some courage.

I TAPPED ADVICE from Russell and Paula combined it with my own hard-earned experience to offer these questions and factors to consider when you are deciding whether it's time to move:

- *Is your house supporting you, or are you supporting it?* Strongly consider moving if your home is keeping you from pursuing goals, furthering your career, or living the lifestyle you want.
- *Has the family changed?* Kids come, grow, and go. Elderly parents move in; couples divorce, lose a spouse, or retire. If your home can accommodate all that, terrific, but if it's no longer a fit for those who live there, a new place might be better.
- *Can you afford to move?* That's the question most people ask. But the better question is: Can you afford not to? Run the numbers but get creative. I thought I was trapped by a big house that I didn't want to sell in a down market, but renting it out and selling half the furniture freed me tremendously.
- *Face the feelings.* People avoid moving and making changes at home they should make because they're afraid of being sad, but sadness is just a feeling, Russell says. Don't

dodge it. Feel the feeling. "It does feel bad when the familiar is missing. People want to live on one side of the line, but if you don't feel sadness, you can't feel joy."

- *Acknowledge the losses, celebrate the gains.* Yes, I miss having my family around the dinner table and the clamor and laughter and tumult. But I can work late, sleep in, not make dinner if I don't feel like it, and know last night's Chinese takeout will still be in the fridge when I get home. Meanwhile, I'm heartened to know that my daughters are off thriving at college and will be home for Thanksgiving and that they know, as I do, that we are family wherever we are. Plus, I have the freedom to create my next best life.

TAKEAWAY

Moving, even for a positive reason, such as a nicer home or a better school, is scary, says author Russell Friedman. But if you conquer your fear, the rewards can be great. "Too many people stay stuck in an unrewarding place because they're afraid of their feelings."

16

Breaking Up with Stuff Is Hard to Do

Help! I Know Better

"'Tis in my memory locked,
And you yourself shall keep the key of it."

—WILLIAM SHAKESPEARE

After I cleared out my parents' home and sold half my furniture before moving, the downsizing continued. My staging situation put me on the move—literally. I moved on average every seven or eight months. The longest I lived in one home was eighteen months—a blessing. The shortest was three months—a curse. This way of life teaches you to pare down: to clean the garage, the closets, and the files and keep only what you really need and want.

Thus, I continually reevaluated everything I owned and asked if my life would be better without it. With every move, I let go of more. Every time, I felt so much better, lighter, less encumbered.

Don't get me wrong—I still fill a twenty-six-foot truck and then some with my stuff, because I need furniture to fill the homes I live in and stage, which are usually around 3,000 square feet. However, the peripheral stuff—the papers, books, clothes, kitchenware, linens, and little-used appliances—has been given a fine sifting.

Still, one would think that someone who has managed to turn moving into an Olympic sport—someone who has endured six moves in four years—would not be slavishly dragging around boxes of stuff she doesn't need, use, or love. Yet I noticed that even on move number six I was still moving boxes vaguely marked "vases, books, business files" from one house to another to park them in the garage, where they would never get opened.

Humbled by my own guilt, like a priest going to confession, I called Mark Brunetz. "What is wrong with me?" I asked. "I know better."

"Everyone has these mystery boxes they move from one house to another and have no idea what's inside," he told me at the start of what turned into a ninety-minute therapy session. "They need to go."

"I know what's in them. I just bypass them because it's faster to move boxes than sort through them."

"Bypass," he said. "Interesting word. What are you avoiding?" Typical Mark: He cuts right to the chase.

"Okay, if you really want to know, it's emotional laziness. Going through stuff detonates a chain reaction of memories. I get a serious case of 'the feels.' You know, you find files from a real estate venture that didn't work out, letters your dad wrote you while you were a kid at camp, photos from a beach house where you stayed with your ex-husband. Each box has stuff that makes you feel bad, or sad, or old, or wistful, and no one's got time for that, so you say to yourself, 'No thank you. I'll just keep the lid on that.'" This is why millions of baby boomers are dealing with two overstuffed households: their parents' and their own.

"You have to grant yourself permission to acknowledge that you're emotionally tied," Mark added. "Then, instead of going around that feeling—or putting it in a box and moving it to deal with later—deal with it, or it gets worse." Meanwhile, just roll with the waves of emotions as you sort.

Observe your feelings and say to yourself, "Oh, there's that unpleasant thought again, that fear of making a mistake or of betraying my loved one, or that feeling of guilt." Then tell yourself, "I can be uncomfortable and not want to do this. That's normal, but this needs to be done, and I can handle it." Here's how:

- *Face the feelings.* Don't be emotionally lazy. Ask yourself what you're avoiding by not opening a box or sorting the papers in a file cabinet and then face it head on, or the situation will mushroom.
- *Don't fret.* "People often ask me if I have ever regretted giving something away," Mark said. "No, I haven't. It's always been the opposite."

- *Build your sorting muscle.* Sorting through your stuff or your parents' takes mental, emotional, and physical effort. But the more you do it, the better you get at it and the easier it gets. "It's like a muscle that's been dormant," he said. "Use it and it gets stronger."

- *Make it a way of life.* Whether you are moving or not, make it a habit to continually sort, purge, and edit your life and your stuff. Then you will create a home filled only with the items you need, use, and love. Furthermore, your stuff won't build to the point where someday you die (I'm sorry!) or you move out of your home and leave your kids or relatives with a job that requires an archaeologist, a bulldozer, and smelling salts. I got that job.

- *Hang on to good stories.* "People think you and I are on a mission to get everyone to get rid of everything," said Mark, who has his grandfather's wallpaper-hanging tools featured in his home, whereas I display my paternal grandmother's rolling pin. "This is not about getting rid of everything. It is about keeping what's really, really important."

I get the rules, but I'm still human. Unless you don't have a soul, and I know some people like that, you probably have what can only be called feelings. In the feelings line, I somehow got an extra helping, which was probably meant for those people lacking them. I often get waylaid by emotions, including when I am confronted with stuff in my home I don't need, use, or love but can't part with.

Yes, even though I've written many columns urging my readers to let go, lighten up, declutter, not hoard, and not cling to stuff just because it was Mom's or Grandma's or their first love's or their first dog's, and even though I understand as well as anyone the psychology behind our attachment to stuff, I still cling.

Both intellectually and through experience, I know that life is better, simpler, freer, and clearer and homes are more beautiful when they contain only belongings that support and nurture us right now and that the rest is best relinquished. But I had a few categories of belongings that were tough to relinquish.

These were items I kept moving from house to house that by my own rules should have been relinquished.

I bared my soul to Mark and shared with him the stories behind several boxes of stuff I was clinging to like wool socks in the dryer. Here's how he helped me unpack what was really in those boxes. His advice helped me let go, and I'm betting it will help you, too.

BOOKS

THE STORY: Being a writer, reader, and book clubber, I have lots of books. When packed for a move, they fill about fifteen banker's boxes. Yes, I have gone through them. Two moves ago I donated 110 books to charity, and by the time I moved to my sixth, and last, staging project I set aside yet another full box to donate. But most I cannot release. They feel like family. But there are just so many, and they weigh on me.

BRUNETZ: "Have you read them?"
ME: "Oh, yes."
BRUNETZ: "Are you going to read them again?"
I PAUSE, AND HE FILLS THE SILENCE: "No. You are on to the next book."
ME: "But they feel like a part of me."
BRUNETZ: "Give them to the closest library or donation center."

THE OUTCOME: I think about this and decide I will meet him halfway and cut my collection by 50 percent.

MY CALENDARS

THE STORY: I have used a paper-based time management system since 1995. Every year, I get a new set of calendar pages along with a neat box labeled to archive my old calendar.

Thus, I have twenty boxes, each about the size of a hardback dictionary, of calendars chronicling every meeting, phone call, and task. I never refer to them; however, I save them, I guess, because they are literally, kind of, my life.

BRUNETZ: "Here's a little gray area. As a writer, you are a chronicler of stories and may find value in that information and need those archives. But let me ask you, why are you hanging on?"

ME: "In case someone asks me, and I hope no one does, what I have done with my life. I can look at my notes."

BRUNETZ: "I could argue that you keep them. But consider paying an intern to scan them into a digital file so they don't take up space."

THE OUTCOME: I probably am not going to scan them because I probably would lose that file, but I will keep them for now.

DIAMONDS

THE STORY: The two half-carat diamonds were from a long-ago relationship back in my early twenties. When the relationship ended, I had the diamonds made into earrings. The post on one earring promptly broke, which I took as a sign. I did not care to have the earrings fixed, and so the diamonds have stayed in a black velvet box for years. I come across them every time I move and think, "I really should do something with these." I told myself that every time. This time I did do something.

I mentioned to Mark that I had recently sold the diamonds to a wholesaler diamond buyer. I worried that he'd say I made a mistake. I knew a wholesaler buyer would not get me top dollar, but selling diamonds to a private party online takes time. I would have had to get the gems certified and deal in a market fraught with fakery and fraud. I didn't want the hassle. I got offers from three diamond buyers in town that ranged from $485 to $600 for the pair. Each buyer acknowledged that the pair would retail for three times that. But I wanted to unlock their value and move on. I decided to use the money toward a trip I am planning with my oldest daughter after she graduates from college.

BRUNETZ: "What you did was fantastic! Why hang on to something that reminds you of something that didn't work? Instead, you unlocked the value and put it toward a new experience with your daughter and a great memory."

THE OUTCOME: I was able to put the $600 in the travel fund for the trip with my daughter.

READERS RESPOND

Although I am not Ann Landers, I get e-mails from readers seeking help resolving deep personal problems—such as what color to paint their kitchens or whether to put wood floors or carpet in their bedrooms—as if I had some know-it-all oracle at my fingertips that could spit out the right answers.

I wish I did.

However, my columns on getting rid of stuff at home generated a lot of good questions. They prompted many stirred-up readers to lay bare their problems about their attachment to things. Then they asked me for answers. Some also shared some excellent solutions. Because their questions may be yours, I share them here, along with my answers.

Dear Marni,

Where do I get rid of the beautiful things I no longer want? The kids don't want them. I don't want to send them to the thrift store. There they might get broken by rough handling or go to some home I don't deem appropriate for things that have meant a great deal to me. Maybe I'm being silly, but it's hard to let go.

—Janice M., San Francisco, CA

Dear Janice,

First, congratulations on deciding to let go. You are halfway to a cleaner home and a clearer life. Now comes the question of where to let the stuff go to. You're not being silly, but ask yourself why you need to "deem" the new home "appropriate."

We're not talking about a child or a pet. These are inanimate objects. Maybe no one will love them as you have. Though that would be nice, it may not be realistic.

If the items are desirable, try personally selling them at your next church bazaar or at a garage sale. Then you can talk to buyers about what they mean to you. If not that, then ask your local thrift or consignment store if you could have a hand in their display.

If you don't clear these items out and your kids don't want them, eventually they or someone will have to deal with them, and they won't do it as well as you will. A lifetime habit of judicious editing is a gift you give your children.

Dear Marni,

I am perfectly willing to discard my mother's, grand-mother's, and even some of my great-grandmother's belongings. My question is, HOW? Do I just throw my grandmother's blouse in the trash? Do I do the same with my mother's memory book from her youth? I even have the clothes my mother wore at her wedding. These items are not suitable for donation, but the idea of putting them in the trash just doesn't feel good. Any suggestions?

—Tina L., Denver, Colorado

Dear Tina,

I have a few suggestions for the clothing. One: Using pinking shears, cut out a square of the fabric and put it under glass with a photo of your relative, where it will serve as a small, cherished reminder. Two: Look up quilting circles in your area and donate the garments to them.

As for the memory book, if it is full of family photos, I would save it. If it is full of letters and photos from people you don't know or it was uniquely personal to your mom but not so much to the family—for example, if it's from her high school days—I would say it has served its useful life as HER memory book, not yours. Try asking your local historical society if they have any interest; many historical societies welcome such items.

Dear Marni,

I agree with much of what you have written, but it occurs to me: What if holding on to extraneous stuff supports and nurtures us right now? I'm not saying that having more stuff makes us more valid, only that if you have a little extra space and you are not moving frequently, is having memorabilia altogether bad? I know it is a balance issue.

—Chris C., Salt Lake City, Utah

Dear Chris,

If you have the space and aren't moving a lot, holding on to stuff is more justifiable than it is for folks who don't have the space and whose stuff compromises their quality of life. So in that respect, your holding on is not doing any harm. Just bear in mind that eventually someone— you or your family—will have to deal with this. Thinning out the cupboards regularly prevents the "stuff snowball" that otherwise forms.

But you raise a more philosophical issue: What if our stuff sustains us now? Certainly, memories and connections to meaningful people and times in our lives do matter and sustain us. Some people, by personality and by circumstance, acquire more memorabilia than others. So here's the question to ask: To what degree are these belongings holding you back? Letting go really does help you grow and move forward. Too many mementos from days gone by—and you should absolutely have some—can create a drag on your life in every sense. Only you can divine the line between too much and just enough.

ALTHOUGH THIS NOMADIC LIFE is not for everyone, it has taught me a lot about what matters.

Being not tethered to a house the last several years has given me a lot of time to think about what I really want in a home. It's a freedom few people have.

I get a do-over, and by not being tied to real estate, I have the freedom to reinvent the next half of my life and decide where I want to live, with whom, and how.

So I dream. City or country? Modern or vintage? House or town home? No yard, big yard?

Most days, I envision an intimate home but not a broom closet. I want an easy keeper with enough usable canvas for me to imprint my soul in three dimensions. I want a place where my growing-up girls, guests, and the dog I plan to have can live in comfort and style. I want to be close to some city life but not so close that I can't see the stars. I want gracious but not grand, lovely but not lavish, pretty not pretentious.

And this for sure: I will not get a bigger house, but I will get a better one for me. I will continue to downsize up. By that I mean, and this is key, that I will live better with less stuff in less space. I will live better knowing that I have everything I need and no more. I will live better knowing that I have all the space I need, but not more than I need. This, my friends, is the very definition of down-sizing up—living better because you have freed yourself of excess.

In Chapter 17, I will share the stories of two couples who are both a few giant steps ahead of me on the bell curve and are realizing that goal.

TAKEAWAY

"Every home has mystery boxes, which when opened release a flood of nostalgia and mixed emotions. While it's tempting to keep the lid on them, tackling them head on means managing the mushroom of memorabilia that will result if you don't." —Mark Brunetz

The Browns and the Switzes

Two Couples Leading by Example

"The greatest wealth is to live content with little."

—PLATO

There are many great reasons for downsizing up—living a better quality life with less in a smaller space—but one of the motives for those in this forward-thinking, downsizing-up group is not wanting to leave their adult children with a fully loaded house. (Mom and Dad, I love you, but seriously? That was a royal pain in the backside.) If you are a young active boomer and have a full house, read closely.

LORI BROWN'S STORY

A talent acquisition executive in Chicago, Lori Brown said good-bye to her 4,000-square-foot home in a lovely suburb to move with her husband to something smaller but in many ways better. In 2013, the Browns—she was fifty-five and he was seventy at the time—moved from their single-family home of twelve years to a luxury condo in a high-rise.

"It wasn't easy to leave," Lori said. "We had a lot of great memories there, but it seemed like it was time."

Leaving got a whole lot easier when they found their new place. The full-service lakefront condo is about 25 percent smaller than their old house, with no yard duties. "We were excited," she said.

"Before, when I thought of people downsizing, I'd think they were compromising, but that's not it at all. We have so many new places to explore. There's nothing sad about it. We made an upgrade."

This is exactly what Kay Morrison, owner of The Occasional Wife, a New Orleans–based company that helps people clear out and organize their homes, characterized as a major trend in the United States today.

"The resistance to downsizing is changing," said Kay, whose downsizing clientele keeps getting younger.

In 2006, when she started her company, which is now in several states, most of her downsizing clients were in their late seventies and eighties.

"Now more are in their sixties," she said. "They want to get this done sooner to simplify their lives, relieve some financial stress, have more freedom, and leave less for their kids to deal with."

"Doesn't all that letting go and living smaller make them feel as if they're, well, winding down?" I asked.

"No, no," said Kay. "They don't see this as the next

step toward death." (Aach! She said the *D* word.) "They see it as the next step toward *freedom*. When they're done, they're ecstatic. . . . Parents always say they don't want to be a burden to their kids, but you're burdening your kids by not going through your stuff."

"I'll say!" I told her. "I will never recover the brain cells, heart muscle, and years off my life that I lost when I cleared out my parents' home."

"One of the best gifts parents can give their children is to take care of all this while they are capable and healthy and can make decisions," said Kay.

The Browns' new place, which overlooks Lake Michigan, is a quick walk to restaurants, shops, and public transportation. "That will make life easier. We'll walk more and get out more."

Sounds like right-sizing to me.

Create Your Criteria

Though everyone's criteria for the ideal home differs, depending on family, work, and lifestyle, here's what the Browns factored into their equation:

- *Must have.* They definitely wanted an urban lifestyle with an easy walk to the action. A big dining area was also a must. "When our family gets together for Sunday dinner, there are fourteen of us," Lori said. "On holidays there can be up to twenty-two." She wanted enough room to gather, eat, watch football, and have the grandkids sleep over.

- *Will sacrifice.* Though Lori wanted an outdoor space where she could put couches and a fire pit, "that's not what we bought," she said. However, the condo complex has a pool, which wasn't on their wish list. Their seven grandchildren, ages four to eighteen, were excited about that. "They will be here every weekend. Now watch our grocery bills soar," she joked.

Net Gains

- *Lower overhead.* "We've been looking for ways to cut our overhead and find better ways to spend our money and time so we can do more traveling," she said. After the move, their house-related expenses will go down by half, she estimates. Property taxes will be one-fourth what they were for their former home.
- *One level.* The house the Browns left was three stories. The new condo is on one level in an elevator building. "We are getting older," she said. "This seemed like a good time to plan for that."

- *Less driving.* For her work downtown, Lori used to spend close to $4,000 a year on parking. Now she can easily take public transportation.
- *More convenience.* Because their former home was outside the city, "once we were home, we stayed. We didn't go out. That has changed," she said.
- *A view.* Lori likes it that her new place is on the third floor with lots of windows so that she can see the treetops as well as Lake Michigan.

"Yes," she said, "we gave up being in a single-family home that we really loved and had put a lot into. But we're moving into a place where we will have a better life. It feels fun. It feels lighter."

THE SWITZES

"My husband and I have very different approaches to saving things," said Lee Switz of Richmond, Virginia, speaking for nine out of ten married couples in the United States.

Am I right?

Lee, who was seventy-two when we spoke in early 2015, had moved just a few months earlier from a 4,900-square-foot, six-bedroom, three-story house where she and her husband had lived for forty of their fifty years of marriage and raised three children. They relocated to a single-story 2,000-square-foot condo less than half that size.

Her husband, Don, age seventy-eight and a semiretired physician, "keeps everything," she said. "I had tried to help him organize his study over the years, and that always led to a conflict. Finally, it got to the point where the space was so cluttered with forty years of his career that he didn't want to work there anymore, and he moved his office to the kitchen."

You can imagine how well that worked out.

Their different approach to stuff was only one reason the Switzes decided that their downsizing would require a mediator.

Enter the move manager. This growing group of professionals steps in when older adults can't downsize alone or would rather not, when the sorting and moving process gets too contentious, or when adult children live hundreds or thousands of miles away or are otherwise unavailable, according to Mary Kay Buysse, executive director for the National Association of Senior Move Managers.

Yes, there's an association.

Not only that. It's growing like cornstalks in the night.

In 2006, when Mary Kay Buysse became executive director for NASMM—which tests, screens, trains, and stamps with approval professionals who help older adults downsize in place or move to a new place—the association had sixty-six move manager members.

By 2015, the association, based in Hinsdale, Illinois,

had nearly a thousand members in forty-six states and Canada. Mary Kay, who has a master's degree in gerontology, attributed that growth not so much to her skill as to changing demographics.

She points to the age wave, which is actually an age tsunami. Between 2010 and 2030, the U.S. population age sixty-five and older will jump by 80 percent. By 2030, one in five Americans will be eighty-five or older. Add to that the fact that families are more spread out than ever and you see why there's a need for her services.

I am actually comforted by the aging of America. Think of all the collective wisdom we'll have.

People like the Switzes are a perfect example of that wisdom.

Their large home was holding them back from what they really wanted to spend their time doing: traveling, going to the theater, reading, listening to music, seeing friends, and visiting their children, Lee Switz told me.

"We were spending so much time and energy cutting the grass and maintaining the garden and the house that we didn't have time to do what we loved," she said.

"We didn't need all that space," she continued. "We spent all our time in the kitchen, the bedroom, and the TV room. We never went into the rest of the house. Every time I paid the electric bill, I would ask myself, 'Why am I heating a house three times larger than we need?'"

Switz researched options for services that help retirees unpack a lifetime's worth of memories and chose Door to

Door Solutions, downsizing relocation specialists in the Richmond, Virginia, area and members of NASMM.

"It was very, very helpful to have an organization come in and help us figure out what to get rid of and then get rid of it for us."

The process—from first meeting with the movers, to moving into their condo, to staging and selling the big family home—took thirteen months, she said. During that time, the service "made dozens of trips, dragging books off to the library, furniture to the auction house, and household items to the thrift store."

Door to Door had a truck and did the heavy lifting. "We didn't want to hurt ourselves," said Lee.

(See what I mean about the wisdom?)

Their children, she said, all in their forties, wanted very little but took a few furnishings. Many of the large pieces of furniture Lee and Don really liked, such as their dining-room table, went to their new place.

But there was much that they let go. "What you learn is that no matter what you have, nobody wants it anymore," she said. "There's no market, and the kids aren't interested."

As they whittled their belongings, the move managers helped them plan space for the new quarters and then not only moved the items but helped them settle in the new condo.

"Unlike regular movers," said Mary Kay, "they don't disappear after the truck is unloaded. They hang pictures and curtains and set up the cable television."

For a fee, of course. Two-thirds of move managers charge between $26 and $60 per hour, while the remaining third charges more than $60 per hour, according to a 2014 NASMM survey of approximately two hundred member organizations. Meanwhile, 42 percent of respondents said they spend from seventeen to thirty-three hours total to complete an average job for their clients, and 39 percent spend more than thirty-three hours (figures were unavailable for the remaining 19 percent).

"The more we got rid of, the better I felt," said Lee. By the time they moved, she felt relieved. Mostly.

"Saying good-bye to the memories is very hard," she conceded. "But now it's wonderful to feel free to travel. With the condo association taking care of things, we can lock the door and leave. It's very freeing. I now spend 90 percent of my time doing what I love."

TIPS TO SMOOTH A MOVE

After many years of working with retirees and empty nesters, here are some insights and pointers Mary Kay Buysse and Kay Morrison have uncovered that make these moves go more smoothly:

- *Create a vision.* Picture what a great downsize looks like. Kay describes it this way: "Everything is easier, simpler, more enjoyable, less hectic, and less stressful. And you have the things around that you love and enjoy most. Downsizing is not sad. It's a time when you can reassess what matters and choose to put around you what you enjoy the most."

- *Attitude—and timing—makes a difference.* Moves to downsize are much easier when people choose to move, as the Switzes did, rather than when the move chooses them, which happens when people become too frail, have an accident, lose a spouse who made independent living possible, or start having cognitive issues.

- *Find the silver lining.* If the move is into assisted living, and not a happening condo as in the case of the Browns and the Switzes, the move at first glance may make it seem that one's independence is shrinking, but it's actually expanding, said Mary Kay. "Going to the right level of care can expand independence and quality of life, and extend life."

- *You are not your kids' attic.* When kids move out, the family house often remains a repository for all their memorabilia: baseball gloves, ice skates, school pictures. "It's not your job to save everything from your children's lives," Kay said. "Box up what belongs to each kid and send it to them." If it's furniture you no longer want but your children do, tell them to claim it now or never. Don't be the family storage locker. Mary Kay adds that a recurring theme she hears from empty nesters is that they wish their adult kids would have claimed their stuff sooner. "For a while it comforts both parties to have the grown child's belongings at home," Mary Kay said. But when the children are in their forties and their scouting badges are still in the basement, it's time to purge.

A NEW GENERATION

Much of the difference in attitude is generational, said Mary Kay Buysse. Many older Americans lived through the depression and World War II, including my parents and Mary Kay's. They were not big acquirers, but they also did not let go. The next two generations were big acquirers but let go more easily.

"Our attitude," said Mary Kay, speaking for those in middle age, "has been if we give something away, we can find it again tomorrow. Because we have more stuff, we're more willing to downsize. We didn't live through an era where coffee and stockings were rationed."

- *Give deadlines.* It's easy for family members not living in the home to put off claiming what they want. Meanwhile, the person on the front lines doesn't want to get rid of stuff because he or she fears someone later saying, "I can't believe you got rid of that!" Issue a deadline. Tell family members the date you plan to have the house cleared out and to let you know by then what they would like or otherwise hold their peace.
- *Use technology.* FaceTime or Skype family members. Walk them through the house as you apply colored stickers with their names on what they want. On little stuff such as tools or jewelry, put the items on a table or in a bag that bears a sticker with their name on it.

     After Mom moved to assisted living, because of her memory issues and the level of care she required, the staff recommended that we keep her jewelry, with the exception of her wedding ring, which she never took off. When sorting it, I first selected the few pieces I wanted. Then Chickie, my sister-in-law, put all the rest on her dining room table and Skyped with my two daughters, who were in separate states, so that they could pick the pieces of their grandmother's they would like. Chickie chose one brooch, and the rest we sold at the estate sale. It all sold within the first hour.

- *Don't do it alone.* When going through old belongings that carry a lot of emotional weight, like the closet of a deceased spouse or parent or even a child's room after the child has moved out, have a close friend or family member with you, said grief expert Russell Friedman. "Touching belongings that trip memories is a huge emotional stimulus," he said. "Stuff is a strong connective device. It's important to have someone to talk to as you unspool the thread that's tied to the stuff."

- *Consider an objective party.* When the items are less emotional, experts in this field recommend having an objective (as in, not a relative) outsider help you for a variety of reasons. They will bring an unbiased clearheadedness. "I always find, when I go to a downsizing situation, an awful lot of blaming about who is the pack rat," said Kay. "Usually, the couple has been together a long time and it's a combination." A third party can neutralize the blaming.

"You want someone who brings an abundance of energy and won't get overwhelmed," she said. Also, Mary Kay added, parents, no matter how old, will always see their children as children. When an adult child takes control, that upsets the equilibrium. "It can get messy." Often what the outsider brings is not only another pair of hands but a compassionate ear.

"It's really about being kind and patient and letting them tell the story of what they're attached to. We come and bring boxes, but also the tissues," Kay said.

- *It gets easier.* Start with the easiest places, said Mary Kay. Clear out the basement, the garage, and the kids' bedrooms. Here's why: Over time you get desensitized to the downsizing process, so it gets easier. "It is easier to get rid of the garden tools than the cookware, so start in the shed."
- *Do the math.* If you are moving to a smaller place, say, from 3,000 square feet to 1,500, figure you'll need to cut your stuff by half or more. To picture what will and won't fit, sketch a floor plan of the new place and then make cutouts of the furniture and arrange it in the sketch. Similarly, Kay suggests making a diagram of the kitchen cabinets. Use sticky notes to indicate where items such as glassware, dishes, and small appliances will go. "When I show clients this is the only shelf they will have for glassware, they get

it," she said. "When they become active in the process, their anxiety disappears."

- *Use hands-on space-planning tools.* These tools, which are available online or can be purchased, can help people see how their furniture will or won't fit. You can virtually "stick" furniture in different spaces to check fit and flow. "When an older adult can see why her seven-foot sofa won't fit, she feels she's participating and arranging her own furniture, and that's a big deal," said Mary Kay.

- *Colored stickers are your best friend.* Get packs of them and make a key: Purple is keep. Yellow means give away. Green goes to a family member. Red is for a garage sale. Go room by room and put stickers on everything. "When you're done, you will have completed one of the hardest parts of the job—making the decisions," said Kay.

- *Give choices.* When you are downsizing a large collection, you don't have to give up the entire curio cabinet. For example, in the case of a well-traveled client who had collected eighty-five teapots from all over the world, Mary Kay said the mover helped the woman select three; then they photographed the rest and put them in an album alongside the three she kept.

NO HOUSE IS FOREVER:
TRANSITION—PLAN FOR IT

When I moved into my house in Colorado in 2003, I naively believed that would be my house forever. Well, here I am in Florida, six moves later, to tell you that no house is forever. Because I was going through my own household upheaval alongside my parents' transition, a financial planning e-pitch I received one day that I normally would have zapped with my spam blocker caught my curiosity.

Although I personally do not feel the need for a financial planner, this was not your typical pitch.

"The recession is the very best thing that happened to Americans," it read. "It got them to rethink their priorities."

I called Guy Hatcher of Southlake, Texas, the financial planner behind the pitch. "Americans got too wrapped up in having things," he told me as we began talking. "They bought into the culture of stuff. Eventually, many saw that the more they got, the less free and happy they felt. The recession has helped them get back to quality, not quantity."

"Is that what happened to you?" I asked, my journalistic nosiness kicking in.

"Like a lot of people who get to be forty-five or fifty and have been successful, I looked up a few years ago and asked, 'This is it?'" said Guy, who was then fifty-two. "I used to believe that having things would bring me respect. But all assets take work. Houses have to be kept up, and that takes time and energy. Whenever I see clients downsize, I see their stress go down."

"After owning four progressively larger houses," I shared, "I like having less house and fewer things."

"You're ahead of most people."

"I love to be ahead," I said. "Even if that means having less."

Ever on the lookout for advice that I can use or that at least will make me feel better, I asked Guy what insights and advice he had for folks facing life and housing transitions, and he said:

- *You are not your stuff.* "Too many people relate who they are to what they own, but we are not our houses or our things," he said. "Besides, what's the point of having a big house if you're no fun and not having fun, if no one's coming over to play cards?" Once people grasp that, letting go gets much easier.

- *Less stuff equals more happiness.* The day Guy hit bottom, he saw that he had lots of material success but was depressed. He started unloading assets, a business, and some land. "As I did, I freed up my life to have more family time, more fun, and more freedom."

- *Get wiser with age sooner.* The importance of things goes down with age, starting at age fifty, he said. "By your eighties, possessions really don't matter." Why do so many people have to live so long before they understand that?

- *Manage expectations.* "The biggest problem our move managers have is getting rid of the excess. The kids and grandkids don't want what the parents or grandparents have been saving for them for years. They don't want the china, silver, crystal, or figurine collections," said Mary Kay. "Yet the parents think these are sizable gifts." Her members try to be straightforward and plant the seed that their stuff isn't worth that much.
- *Know what you love.* And take it with you. I assure you, most material belongings really don't matter. But some do. Look around your home and ask yourself what brings you comfort and what would break your heart to leave behind. The latter list should be short. But what's left will help you define your style, your person, your sense of place. For me, it was my French writing desk, a few paintings, and a four-poster bed that was my parents' wedding bed. For my parents, it was their favorite blue chairs, their blue-and-white dishes, and select pieces of art and family photos reflecting their life.
- *Put the same things the same way.* My sister-in-law re-created the top of my parents' dresser exactly the way they had arranged

it at their old home. She even hung the art around it in the same way.

- *Ask the kids.* Have your children tell you what they want. Don't assume they want anything unless you ask and they say so. Many parents make the default decision not to purge because they have deluded themselves into believing their kids will want the twenty-year-old blender. They don't.
- *Allow time.* It took forty years to build a home. You don't have to dispose of it all in two weekends. Give the process the dignity it deserves. But don't wallow or you'll lose momentum. Be thoughtful and acknowledge the sentiment, but keep moving.

TAKEAWAY

As Mary Kay Buysse notes, "When downsizing, clashes between couples or between parents and their adult children are common. It can get messy. An objective expert can smooth the process." If each generation can understand and respect the other's attitudes and have some awareness of the reasons for wanting or not wanting items, together they can come to a rational result.

PART FOUR

For Keeps

KEEPSAKE: Something that one keeps because of the memories it calls to mind.

18

Archival Storage

How to Keep Stuff for Almost Ever

"Is there none such, nowhere known some, bow or brooch or braid or brace, lace, latch, or catch or key to keep back beauty . . . from vanishing away?"

—GERARD MANLEY HOPKINS

I am not done yet. I may never be.

Yes, I got my parents' house cleared out. I sold, salvaged, saved, and scrapped. While workers made improvements to get it ready for market (you'll read about that in the next section), I still had to deal with . . . the garage.

It was a way station where I had temporarily off-loaded those family keepsakes that probably would have required me to take a deeper dive to select what exactly would move into long-term preservation. Stacks of slides in carousels, military discharge papers, marriage certificates, and diplomas remained until someone (me) sifted through with an archaeologist's attention and a genealogist's care (see Chapters 10 and 11).

The earthmover methods I had been using would not work now.

Besides, if these archive-worthy items were going to last

another lifetime, I knew they'd need special handling. I parked them in the garage, putting off the project until the house sold.

When it did, I suddenly needed to get serious about saving for keeps.

My brother took all the slides—to his house.

My job as family historian by default was to preserve forever what I decided, after all the whittling, mattered.

But save how? Anyone who has ever opened a box of old precious possessions and found mouse turds, dead bugs, yellowed brittle pages, or stains so established that they had mortgages knows what it means to store things wrong.

I needed to figure this out.

Coincidentally, right after I returned to Florida from my long week at ground zero, I learned that back in my hometown of Orlando, The Container Store® was opening its sixtieth store that week. As a member of the media, I was invited for a sneak peek before opening day. I told my tour guide I was particularly interested in archival storage.

They had exactly the right storage solution.

Although I do not often buy stuff for my stuff, stores that sell storage solutions such as The Container Store, Bed Bath & Beyond®, and The Home Depot®, among many others, provide helpful and attractive tools to make your world better ordered.

"We have been working with our customers on storage solutions for over thirty-five years," said Karen Hartman, sales trainer for The Container Store. "We have given this a lot of thought."

"Perfect," I said. "Lay it on me." We'll get to her advice in a moment, but first I want to introduce you to another archival expert I uncovered.

If I do anything well, it's learning and benefiting from the hard thinking of others. "Excuse me, may I borrow that intelligence?" That is pretty much how I get through life.

Taking matters further, which we journalists tend to do, I found one of the nation's leading experts in saving stuff for almost ever.

Don Williams is the senior conservator at the Smithsonian Institution, that museum chain in Washington, D.C., where you'll find things like Dorothy's ruby slippers and the lightbulb Thomas Edison invented. Don's job is to make old stuff last.

"But no matter what we do," he told me, "everything turns to dust."

That did not cheer me up.

A book he cowrote, *Saving Stuff*, helps people do that. The people who grab this book are the ones who have uncovered a stack of photos in which they could no longer tell the men from the women (I'm talking about photos taken before the 1960s), stumbled across a grandmother's wedding dress and felt the lace crumble in their hands, or found the 300-year-old family Bible soaked in the basement where a pipe broke. These are people who wonder what they might do differently from now on.

I then realized that Don was fighting my fight, though probably with more success. He actually has made a career out of stalling the inevitable. And he was generous enough to share his preservation principles so that real people, not just museums, could extend the lives of keepsakes.

"Museums know what they're doing and have resources," he said. "I want to help families and communities preserve their heritages."

Then he added: "Though nothing lasts [forever], unless we can change the nature of the universe, we can help make things last longer."

That's the spirit! I wondered if his techniques would work for skin, as I noticed mine suddenly had about as much rebound as a twenty-year-old bathing suit.

Although degeneration is inevitable, with a few simple practices and a good dermatologist, you can slow the process, he assured me.

HOW TO STORE STUFF FOR KEEPS

For folks who want to protect and preserve their heirlooms, collectibles, and other keepsakes, Don Williams and Karen Hartman offer this advice:

- *Edit, edit, edit.* Then preserve. We all agree, right? Store only what is really, really important. But once you've sifted artifacts from debris, store it properly.
- *Know your enemies.* The big ones are heat, bugs, vermin, bad plumbing, light, and dirt.

(They can't be too great for your skin either.)
These are the most common enemies that
destroy over time. Of course, the less common,
but even more destructive enemies—fire and
flood—can destroy in minutes.

- *Clean it up.* Don't store dirty stuff. Have
garments professionally cleaned. Remove
any embellishments, such as pins, which also
can leave stains.
- *Pick the right place.* Most people stick
heirlooms in the basement or the attic—bad
choices. Basements flood or get mildewy.
Attics get hot. And garages are the worst.
Witness my old ice skates, the toes of
which—I learned after sticking my hand
inside—a resourceful mouse had used for a
nest. Pee-eww!

"They combine unregulated temperature,
exposure to the elements, and vehicle
pollution," said Don. If the basement is the
best you can do, be sure that the structure
is sound, that you don't store items directly
under water pipes, and that you keep them
up on palettes. The only precious items you
can store safely in the attic are ones that
can't burn, like ceramics, china, and crystal.
For most other items, cool is best. For every
18 degrees Fahrenheit, reaction rates for

deterioration double. An item stored at 88 degrees will break down twice as fast as one stored at 70 degrees, said Don.

- *Use the right container.* Store keepsakes in sealed plastic (polypropylene or polyethylene) opaque (not clear) tubs. Clean the inside of the tub first with rubbing alcohol. The right, properly cleaned tub will prevent the major causes of deterioration: moisture, contaminants, pests, and light. Toss in an envelope of dry-activated charcoal, the kind available at pet stores for fish tanks. Charcoal will absorb odors and pollutants and create a chemically controlled microclimate. (Note: This also works for stinky shoes.) Safes are a good place for important documents, and can often withstand fire or water damage.

- *Go archival.* Look for archival labels when selecting storage supplies. Karen explained that *archival* means it's treated to protect keepsakes from the ravages of acid, dust, dirt, pests, and light so that when the items are stored for a long time, they will stay in good shape.

- *Treat acid as your enemy.* Though they seem harmless, paper and wood contain acids that will cause papers, photos, and fabric to yellow and get brittle over time. They also contain lignin, a kind of cellulose that binds wood but produces acid as it deteriorates. Cedar chests, long used for storage, have natural tannic acid in them. "That old dresser drawer is an unsafe environment," Karen said. Archival storage containers are acid-free or acid-neutral, meaning they have had the acid buffered.

- *Consider it a long-term investment.* Because these are not your ordinary boxes, archival storage items cost more. You pay for acid-free treatment and sturdier, reinforced corners that keep boxes from being crushed when other boxes are stacked on them, which you know will happen. Prices can range from $6 to $45 for one of these boxes, depending on size and material, and this may encourage you to be even more selective about what you keep.
- *File under forever.* Treasures come in all sizes. So does archival storage. Archival-quality boxes come in a dozen sizes, right for files, photos, and garments. Store paper items such as birth certificates, marriage licenses, immigration documents, and military discharge papers in archival file or garment boxes.
- *Use protective plastic.* You'll also want acid-free plastic for storing photos, CDs, or

DVDs, especially those which contain family photos. Archival plastic sleeves also keep baseball card and stamp collections from degenerating.

- *Don't forget the tissue.* "If you buy an archival box but wrap items in paper that is not acid-free, you've defeated the purpose," said Karen. This is true for the envelopes and folders that contain these items. Make sure they are acid-free.

- *Use the right climate.* Avoid light as well as excessive heat and moisture. Light damage is cumulative and irreversible. Whether it comes from the sun or from artificial lighting, whether it's direct or indirect, light wears things down. For museums, Don and other conservators determine the total amount of lumens a painting can receive per day. When the exposure hits that limit, the painting goes into the dark for a while.

- *Stuff and wrap.* Before putting the lid on, use acid-free tissue to fill sleeves and soften folds in garments. You want no hard creases, because that is where a garment will break down. Once it has been stuffed, wrap the whole garment in acid-free paper so that no part is exposed. If you store more than one garment in a box, put tissue between the items.

- *Put a name on it.* Once you've carefully packaged, label the box. Most archival storage boxes have a label area on the end.
- *Use the right handling.* When you do want to appreciate one of your collectibles, say, old letters or an old baptism gown, wash your hands; don't wear skin creams or perfumes, which are contaminants; and wear clean gloves.
- *Pick the right stuff.* Don encourages people to create a "museum of you." Obviously you'll want to preserve items that have value in the marketplace, such as that Stradivarius violin. But other items, including important papers such as birth and marriage certificates, house titles, wills, and other legal documents, have value to families for generations. Also important are things that define a person's passions. Don, for instance, values his father's work apron, which no one else could appreciate.

TAKEAWAY

"Each person has to decide what belongs in his or her family museum and then protect it. What remains is the fabric and memory of society." —Don Williams

19

Handle with Care

Shipping the Heirloom China and Other Breakables

"Make us heirs of all eternity."

—WILLIAM SHAKESPEARE

I had just stepped out the door for a morning jog when I saw a blizzard of pink packing peanuts swirling and skipping down the street. What idiot did that? I wondered.

My stomach turned inside out when I realized the eye of the storm was my trash can. Moments before, it had been filled to the brim with the pink packing material that had cradled my mother's china on its sentimental journey from California to Florida.

The trash collectors had just been by. It was a windy day. And I had instantly become *that neighbor*! I can't stand people like me.

I dashed down the street and began chasing hundreds, perhaps thousands, of pink peanuts, asking myself for the zillionth time: How did I get into this mess?

(Yes, I now know, thanks to my smart readers who wrote to tell me I should have taken the peanuts to a packing store for recycling. But of course! Insert forehead smack here. I didn't think of that, I am embarrassed to say.)

Anyway, the sudden need for my parents' china started just before Thanksgiving, six months after I had cleared out and sold the family home. My brother had been graciously storing the china, along with a few items I was going to "get around to" shipping from his home to mine on the opposite coast. That moment came as I was setting the Thanksgiving table and suddenly got choked up. A wistful wave of nostalgia washed over me as I flashed on all those holiday dinners around my mother's table and her delicate, ivory china with its hand-painted gold pattern.

Three thousand miles away, I was trying to create a new life and make my own meaningful traditions after the ending of my long marriage. I suddenly needed that family china like I needed oxygen. Only it was sitting in a box in my brother's garage in California, not doing anyone any good.

You'll recall that after I had cleared out my parents' home, I had brought home some jewelry, glassware, and an oil painting but had held off on the silver and china. I wasn't ready emotionally (the memories!) or physically (where to put it?) or financially (the packing, insuring, and shipping costs!) to deal with the twelve place settings.

But as I set the Thanksgiving table, I did some mental math, which sounds like a hand-cranked pencil sharpener, and figured that I probably have had more Thanksgivings than I will have.

Forget what anyone tells you. This is the definition of midlife. And it is a crisis. Suddenly, my desire for Mom's china became a stage-five obsession not seen since the days of my pregnancy cravings: *I need a barbecue chicken pizza NOW!*

"Please, send the china," I said to my sister-in-law, Chickie, over the phone. She took the boxes straight to Art, the owner of a local shipping store in Culver City, California, who promptly panicked.

If you want to send a shipper's vital signs into the ozone, just say "heirloom china." An all-points bulletin goes out to delivery trucks nationwide, and the entire transportation network goes on red alert. No two boxes of china can travel on the same truck for the same reason that the president and the vice president can't fly together. Then, the packer corners the market on pink peanuts.

Art, a certified packing expert, and his crew, who happen to be his kids, took the heirloom china job as seriously as a brain tumor. Several days later, I received three boxes the size of microcars and a smaller fourth box that held the silver.

The boxes were so thoroughly packed that you could have dropped them from a freeway overpass and had them knocked around by speeding traffic and the dishes would have been intact. Only delivery by armored car could have offered more protection.

I asked Art how he did it so you, too, can wrap and pack fragile valuables like a pro. He replied:

- *Pad all the parts.* "When shipping breakables, individually wrap each piece with bubble wrap until you can't feel any edges," said Art, who used several layers of small-bubble wrap on each dish. Next, put a layer of peanuts on the bottom of the box. Layer in wrapped dishes so they're not touching; add another layer of peanuts and then more dishes. Once filled, overstuff the box with more peanuts so nothing moves.
- *Box the box.* Art then put that box in another box that was two inches bigger all around, and filled the gap with more peanuts.
- *Assume rough handling.* When packages ship by ground, they typically go from truck to truck and "can be thrown around quite a bit," Art said, "even when they say 'fragile.'" Picture boxes being dropped from a height of three feet and pack accordingly.
- *Nix the newspaper.* The most common mistakes Art sees self-packers make are wrapping breakables in paper and leaving too much room in the box. "When you grab a box, you shouldn't feel the contents moving," he said. "But customers bring their china in that way and think it's ready to ship." Most shippers are good about honoring insurance, but they may want to inspect the packing to

see why an item broke. If the items were not packed properly, it would not be the shipper's fault.

- *Insure it.* Shipping companies offer varying degrees of insurance. With UPS®, for example, each box is automatically insured for $100. For $1.50 more per box, you can buy an additional $100 of protection.
- *Be prepared for sticker shock.* This kind of packing doesn't come cheap. Art said he usually can pack an eight-piece place setting of dishes in two boxes and charges $100 per box. Shipping and insurance are added to that. To pack, ship, and insure our four boxes cost $500. When I asked Art if perhaps he overpacked, he asked me, "Was anything broken?" No, I told him. "Then the job was perfect," he said. Can't argue with that.

That Christmas (and every holiday since) my table was a beautiful, if sentimental, blend of old and new: Mom's gold-rimmed china with my plain ivory, her silver with my crystal. Layering Mom's fine china (Sōkō china, Random Harvest pattern), which Dad bought in Japan in 1952, on mine lets me create a table that keeps family memories and traditions very much in the present.

I discarded the packaging.

And that is how one recent morning, for love, for family,

and so I wouldn't make the neighbors mad, I was trolling through neighbors' yards and streets like a stray dog, chasing that which was fleeting.

P.S. Please recycle your peanuts.

> **TAKEAWAY**
>
> When packing things that matter to ship, this is the question: Is it packed and padded so tightly and so well that a harried truck driver could drop the package from a height of three feet to the asphalt street without breaking it? You must answer yes.

PART FIVE

The Biggest Sale of All

HOMESTEAD: A house, especially a farmhouse, with adjoining land; property qualifying as a person's home providing survivorship rights for spouse and children; the place where one's home is.

20

Selling the Homestead

Not Suffering Fools Kindly

> *"The secret of getting started is breaking your complex, overwhelming tasks into small, manageable tasks, and then starting on that first one."*
>
> —MARK TWAIN

Maybe because I was the youngest in my family or maybe because I'm five foot three and have a voice like Snow White, I tend to lash out like a cornered rattlesnake when someone doesn't take me seriously.

I will take good-natured teasing, a friendly disagreement, moderate proselytizing, or even a heavy-handed agenda, but patronize me and you'd be better off bullwhipped.

A Southern California real estate agent whom we'll call Mr. Lowball found that out firsthand. He played the "there there little lady you can't possibly understand the big complicated world of home sales" card with me.

Oh, yeah?

At issue was the pricing of my parents' home.

BACK AT THE HOME FRONT, I had more work to do on my sentimental journey with a mission. The house, now cleared, needed to be sold. As in many estates, the house was the major asset, and liquidating it would go a long way toward shoring up my parents' liquid assets and savings, providing a base for their long-term care.

Frankly, my father believed that Mom would outlive him and that his remaining days weren't many. He could go in peace if he knew the home's equity had been freed up for her. I needed to do this and do the best job I could—for him. The responsibility felt greater than selling my children.

Knowing that getting the most we could for the house was the ultimate goal in the weeks before I came to town, I contacted a couple of real estate agents.

"We're not in a hurry," I told Mr. Lowball, a fellow whom my parents knew and had asked me to consult. "We'd like to get as much as we can for it."

My parents bought the one-story ranch on one-third of an acre for $24,000 in 1964 and had long since paid it off. Remember, this is Southern California near the coast, where prices now defy common sense.

I had looked over recent sales in the neighborhood and taken the virtual tours. I had a sense of what the place should sell for.

I asked Mr. Lowball what he'd list the house for "as is" and also the price if it was fixed up. (Though in good repair, the house needed cosmetic help.)

I itemized the improvements I had in mind: Scrape the cottage cheese ceilings, take down the flowered wallpaper, paint the interior and the kitchen cabinets, put in new flooring, replace the wimpy baseboards, and trade dated light fixtures for recessed cans and dowdy drapes for wood blinds.

Mr. Lowball (I bet you can tell where this is going) came back with an as-is price so low that a monkey could have gotten it at a pawn shop: $425,000. I know that sounds like a lot, but not by coastal California standards. His fixed-up estimate was even more ridiculous and clearly was intended to discourage the effort so that he could nab a quick sale.

Given his "extensive" experience, he said, the improvements "if all were done in good taste" (excuse me?) would cost around $30,000 and take months. The upgrades would boost the selling price by only $25,000 at most, and so we'd lose money, he said. Forget it.

Ba-lo-ney. Did the guy think I had the IQ of oatmeal?

I called my good friend Bill Wood, a Yorba Linda, California, real estate agent and longtime family friend. Bill owns fifty-nine homes that he has fixed up and rents, so he can fix places up in his sleep.

Unlike Mr. Lowball and many real estate agents who encourage homeowners to sell their property as is, Bill said that if we updated the place and didn't overspend, we'd net more and sell faster.

"What would it take?" I asked. We ran through the improvement list.

"One month and $15,000."

"How much more would we get?"

"Put in $15,000 and you'll get close to $550,000," he said.

"A fourth-grader can do that math."

"Plus," he said, "when a home looks new and move-in ready, buyers are less likely to ask you to drop your price for a paint or carpet allowance."

I pushed up my sleeves. "Let's go," I said.

"No way!" came the chorus from friends, family, and those in real estate. "You can't bring this place into the twenty-first century that fast for that price!"

Oh, yeah? Watch.

I coolly confronted Mr. Lowball with this finding.

Trip. Cough. Sputter. Backpedal. Tune change. He shot back a pathetic apology and upped the sales price by another $25,000 to $475,000 after improvements.

Too late. The fact that he would take advantage of my parents to make a quick sale made my ears smoke. I'll work with someone else, thank you.

I ran this by Bill, who'd heard it all before.

"For most homeowners, their home is their biggest asset. For an agent, it's just a listing," he said.

To an agent making a 3 percent commission, the difference between selling a home for $300,000 and selling it for $330,000 is the difference between making $9,000 and making $9,900. Although $900 may not be worth the extra time and effort to an agent, for a homeowner $30,000 can be huge.

I know there are many good and honest real estate agents. I have worked with them. But every profession— including real estate—has its sleazeballs. And sellers need to look out for them.

Bill gathered estimates for me and said all the work could be done in three weeks.

I told Dad the plan.

"Are you sure we need to do all that? Shouldn't we let the new buyers paint and carpet?" he asked.

"Dad, trust me. Let me do what I do," I said.

"Go for it," he said.

By the time I came to town, I had crews lined up like 747s on the runway: the painters, the flooring crew, a finish carpenter, and a handyman who would replace window treatments, light fixtures, and faucets. They would strip wallpaper, scrape ceilings, replace baseboards, paint walls and cabinets, and put down new floors. I would have to make quick design decisions and fret a lot.

True remodeling never does run smoothly. The project would have been nerve-wracking enough if my money were at stake. But this was my parents' money, their nest egg.

But I trusted my instincts and Bill's advice. Finding that sweet spot—the level of improvement that would help the home sell faster, net the most money, and eliminate reasons for buyers to lowball me—was the key to getting the best price.

WHAT TO FIX WHEN FIXIN' TO SELL

I combined my home-design experience with Bill's to come up with this list of what to consider doing to improve—but not overimprove—a property you're fixing to sell:

- *Be objective.* Many homeowners, my parents among them, have lived in their houses so long that they stop noticing that the finish has worn off the door handles, the paint looks grimy, and traffic patterns are embedded in the carpet. Walk through the home with fresh eyes. List what needs improving. "Most buyers don't have a lot of imagination," Bill said. "If the place has dated finishes and looks run down, in the buyer's mind it will always look that way."
- *Start at the curb.* The property needs to look clean and appealing when you drive up.
- *Modernize.* Even if your home is fifty years old, buyers want updated interiors. "The age of a house can't change, but freshening up the interior with new paint and flooring can make it feel like a new home," said Bill. That's the feeling buyers want.
- *Tackle the interior.* Strip that wallpaper and paint the walls in current neutrals—taupe, gray, and sage. Scrape popcorn ceilings.

(It's never coming back.) Replace worn flooring with neutral carpeting, wood, or engineered wood laminate.

- *Improve kitchens and baths.* Updating fixtures and counters can reap big gains. Money carefully spent in kitchens and baths is well invested. The trick is to not overdo by the standards of the neighborhood.
- *Keep the style consistent.* Don't force a Tuscan interior on a cute little cottage. Stay true to the architecture.
- *Bring on the moldings.* Moldings are cheap and add instant quality, my advisers agreed. Bigger baseboards, crown moldings, and wainscoting all add value.

WHAT TO KEEP IN MIND WHEN PLANNING HOME IMPROVEMENTS

When you are hiring workers, don't assume that there's not much fluctuation in prices. You can really save if you shop and compare prices for the identical work. Also, talk to a few agents. It pays to be picky with your agent, too. If you sense that an agent is pushing you to do what's best for him or her, not you, back away. Look for agents who will sell your home as if it belonged to their parents.

FIXING TO SELL: OLD HOUSE, NEW LOOK

Once empty, the 1,800-square-foot California ranch house looked even more tired than before. The furnishings had buffered the facts that the carpet had seen more miles than a foot army, and the wallpaper was more dated than a bouffant hairdo.

I looked around the home I grew up in, and instead of seeing a refuge where I once tanked up on food, sleep, clean clothes, and abundant parental love and advice; played hide-and-seek; and blew out lots of birthday candles, I tried to see it through a buyer's eyes.

Boy, did that change my perspective.

Bill was right. As we walked the emptied-out house together, we agreed that besides the carpet and wallpaper, the cottage cheese ceilings, and the dowdy drapes, we needed to replace the bathroom counters and shower doors, which were also original.

The fix list grew faster than kids.

Bill's contacts and my ability to make quick design decisions on a budget made us a formidable pair.

In that nine-day year I was in town, after clearing the house and having the estate sale, I selected paint colors, carpets, engineered wood flooring, tile, hardware, and window coverings. (This is more proof that a task will expand or contract to fill the amount of time you have.) The rest I did by puppet strings from Florida.

Bill coordinated the crews in February 2013. One month later, we were ready for market.

Here's What We Did and What We Spent

- *Good-bye, wallpaper.* The flowered wallpaper throughout was cozy, quaint, and just right for its time; that is, back in the day when Doris Day was hot and Elvis was cool. Today's buyers want a fresh, neutral, but not boring palette to build on. We stripped the paper, retextured the walls, and painted them a soft beige; we painted doors and trim an elegant off-white.
- *See ya, cellulite ceilings.* Whoever came up with the idea of coating smooth ceilings with stuff that looks like cottage cheese should be covered in the stuff from head to toe and made to stand in a public square. I heard the angels sing the "Hallelujah Chorus" when they finally came down. Best improvement ever.
- *Farewell, floors.* The house's floors were a patchwork: blue carpet in the master, yellow in my old room, green in my brother's, light brown in the living areas. The kitchen linoleum dated back to the Eisenhower administration. It looked as bad as it sounds.

Without a moment's hesitation, I had all the flooring torn out. In its place, we installed engineered wood laminate: four-inch planks of dark brown antique teak in the entry, living room, family room, kitchen, and laundry. (I love real wood floors, but their much higher cost would have cut too far into the profits.) Then we put a low-pile carpet in a neutral light wheat color in the bedrooms and tiled the two previously carpeted (ick!) bathroom floors. Next, we replaced the very underwhelming baseboards with four-inch moldings painted off-white.

- *Cover those cabinets.* Replacing the cabinets also would have blown the budget, but the home's dark grainy wood cabinets and crusty bronze hardware looked better when Nixon was in the White House. To spiff them up, we sanded and painted them inside and out. Because the freshly painted cabinets then made the tired, rusty vent hood over the stovetop look even worse, we replaced it.

- *It hinges on hardware.* Metal matters. And it must look new if it's going to attract buyers. I ditched all the original and heavily worn

bronze knobs, pulls, hinges, and handles
and replaced them with hardware in brushed
nickel.

- *Catch up those counters.* Now that the main
bathroom had new paint, knobs, and tile
flooring, the laminate counter and original
sinks cried, "Replace me!" We tiled the
counter, put in new nickel faucets and towel
bars, and replaced the sinks and toilets in
both baths. In the master bathroom, we
traded a rickety glass and aluminum door to
the commode for café doors.

- *Can the lights.* We swapped the large
fluorescent kitchen light for six can or
recessed lights, and the brass bathroom light
fixture for one in brushed nickel.

- *Ditch the drapes.* After removing the dowdy
drapery, we left the wood-paned windows
undressed, which let in light and garden
views. Over the aluminum windows, we
hung two-inch white wood blinds. They
finished the windows and provided privacy
and light control, yet new owners would be
able to add drapes if they wanted, to suit
their decor.

YOU DID ALL THAT FOR WHAT?

Paint, remove wallpaper, scrape ceilings	$ 7,150
Laminate floors, carpets, four-inch baseboards	$3,835
Floor tile	$106
Wood blinds	$695
Six canned lights	$175
Stovetop vent hood	$240
Bathroom light fixture	$100
Bath counter materials	$150
Two bath sinks	$80
Two nickel faucets	$60
Towel bars	$40
Two toilets	$196
Café doors	$150
*GFCI protected outlets	$40
New wall plates throughout	$40
Handyman, six days	$1,200
TOTAL:	$14,257

*Ground fault circuit interrupter

Meanwhile, at the assisted-living center, Dad, now ninety and on oxygen because his lungs were shutting down, stayed informed of every step in the transaction. He was riveted, and frankly, his interest kept him alive. Dad's mind was sharp as ever, but he was losing the fight to lung disease, the result of a thirty-year smoking habit he picked up in the service and kicked in his early fifties.

Now, because of recurring pneumonia, which I learned he didn't catch but developed, Dad needed to move into the center's hospital, where he could receive full-time medical and respiratory care. Because Mom couldn't be in the apartment alone, she was transferred to the memory garden, where residents who have memory problems live with specially trained caregivers.

It was the first time in sixty-two years of marriage they had lived apart. We all ached with sadness.

TAKEAWAY

To get an old home ready for the next generation of buyers, we put it through a time machine. The goal was to sell fast at the highest price by giving buyers fewer reasons to say no.

21

Going, Going, Gone

Five Offers, Two Letters, One House

"Where we love is home—home that our feet may leave, but not our hearts."

—OLIVER WENDELL HOLMES SR.

The five offers in forty-eight hours to buy my parents' house bowled me over and provided proof that I had made the right choice with regard to the improvements. Dad stayed in the loop at every turn, following along with the attention he once gave Zane Grey novels.

But what really did me in were the letters.

Two of the buyers submitted their offers with photos of themselves and letters professing their love for the four-bedroom California ranch house, which I was sure no one could love as much as I had. I was a goner.

"I haven't seen anything like this in a long time," said Bill.

"They wrote letters?"

"You probably shouldn't read them."

"Can we sell the house to more than one buyer?" I felt seriously bad about picking just one buyer and turning down four.

See, these weren't just offers; they were great offers. Three were for $15,000 over the asking price, which we had set high at $535,000. (Take that, Mr. Lowball.)

One came in at asking, and one came in $10,000 below asking, but with a 90 percent cash down payment.

I would like to pause here to let the record reflect that the multiple offers confirmed that the $15,000 I strategically spent on the makeover paid off, as I'd hoped, in a faster sale at a higher price than we would have gotten if we'd sold as is. Much higher, meaning a net gain of nearly $100,000.

Not braggin' . . . just sayin'.

But back to my plight. Now, if I had put in a full-price offer on a home within hours of its going on the market, I would assume I had it. Yet the full-price offer was in fourth place.

Although part of me was ecstatic, of course, I also hated to disappoint those earnest buyers. I know what it's like to want a house so badly that you fall asleep at night arranging furniture in your head and continue arranging right on into your dreams.

I know what it's like to get swept away with visions of pulling into the driveway and unloading groceries in your new digs, hosting family and friends there, assigning bedrooms to the kids, telling the dog all about the yard and getting his hopes up, and nesting so intensely that you're practically laying eggs.

Then, poof! The deal caves like a hot cake in a cold draft.

House love, like human love, can be so capricious.

After Bill recapped the offers, we decided to turn down the two lowest ones (sorry!) and ask the three remaining buyers, whose above-asking offers were all within $1,000 of one another, to make their best and final offers.

Two raised their price by $10,000, the third by $5,000.

That was when, against Bill's advice, I read the letters. "We love your home and can see ourselves happy there for many years to come. . . . The backyard, location, and neighborhood will provide a safe and happy environment for our kids to play and grow," one buyer in the finals wrote.

Attached was a picture of a family of four, not unlike mine several decades back. They were standing in front of a backstop. The boy, age three, wore his tee-ball uniform and a baseball glove while the mom held his four-month-old sister.

Another couple, also in the play-offs, wrote, "From the moment we pulled up, we were instantly sold. . . . We could easily picture the two of us and our little one in the living room in front of the fireplace . . . and having family and friends over for barbecues in the backyard."

They included their eighteen-month-old wedding picture and the news that they were expecting their first child.

"They're killing me!" I said.

"Told you not to read them," Bill said.

"What do we do now?"

"We go with the most qualified buyer."

"You mean the one most likely to run the ball over home plate?" I said.

"There's a lot more to an offer than price."

In the end, we accepted the second-highest offer, the one $5,000 lower than the other two, because that buyer scored higher on what else matters (see below); the final sale was $555,000. Dad got my call from his hospital bed. I could hear the smile in his voice as he kept saying over and over, "Five, five, five."

THE MAKINGS OF AN OFFER

Bill and I considered the three upgraded offers, weighing the following factors, which may help you if you're ever faced with multiple offers or are competing for a hot property:

- *Price.* The amount of the offer is easy to fixate on, but higher is not always better.
- *Down payment.* The winning buyer was putting 20 percent down and so had to finance only 80 percent. The other two buyers were planning to put down 10 percent and 5 percent, respectively. Of course, I was partial to the 90 percent cash-down buyers, but their purchase price was too low.
- *Loan.* All three buyers had been preapproved for loans. However, two were getting FHA (Federal Housing Administration) loans, which have more red tape; the ultimate buyer

was getting a conventional loan, which tends to imply better overall credit.

- *Escrow.* We wanted a thirty-day escrow, the period of time when the house goes under contract and both parties get their financial ducks in a row and make their inspections to be sure they really want to go through with this. A lot can happen during an escrow that will cause a deal to go awry and not close. Each party agreed to that time line. But if one had needed a longer escrow, that would have been a drawback.

- *Reserves.* Bill looked at the buying parties' bank statements to see how much money they would have left after the purchase. A buyer with healthy reserves is more attractive to lenders and sellers. Unlike the buyer whose offer we accepted, the two runners-up, though they qualified for the loan, would have been more stretched financially.

- *Contingencies.* The winning buyer had sold a house, and it had closed escrow. They had cash from that sale in the bank and were ready to move. One runner-up had a house in escrow that needed to close. The third was a first-time buyer borrowing money from parents. We favored the buyer with no strings attached.

- *Love letters*. Though Bill was immune to the heartstring tactics, the letters and photos did make a difference to me. Much as I wanted to sell the place to all who loved my childhood home, the little slugger's family got the home run. I hoped the little girl would have my room.

GETTING TO CLOSING: FROM OFFER ACCEPTED TO DEAL DONE

After *you're right*, my next two favorite words are *escrow closed*.

Ask anyone who's sold a house: The journey between offer accepted and escrow closed is akin to carrying live explosives across a minefield.

It all can blow up at any step.

A loan falls through. An appraisal falls short. The roof caves in with the inspector on it. A missing person is on the title and has a lien against the house. You discover you're on an Indian burial ground.

Sellers beware.

If I have learned anything the hard way, it's that nothing makes you look like a fool faster than running ahead of yourself on the rope bridge of presumption. Just as agreements can go sideways between a marriage proposal and the altar, escrows can fall apart after an offer is accepted, sending a home seller back to square one jilted, disillusioned, and abandoned.

To prepare themselves, sellers must first understand what the fuzzy, legal-sounding terms *in escrow* and *under contract* really mean.

Translation: Buckle up, doll face. Light the prayer candle, put a penny in your shoe, and don't count your chickens because this here house deal can slide all over the ice pond before it gets to the other shore, if it ever does.

Thirty days after we accepted the offer for $555,000 from the little slugger's family, escrow closed on April 9, 2013.

The process taught me again the importance of having a great agent. Anyone can snag a buyer. Skill closes the sale. Bill headed off problems before they could derail the deal.

After our escrow closed, I asked Bill, who has thirty years' experience buying and selling houses, how many houses fall out of escrow.

As many as one in five, he said. But 80 percent of houses that open escrow undergo some turbulence.

From Sold to Closed

To get from offer accepted to escrow closed, here are the hurdles sellers must clear, a sampling of what can go wrong, and ways to minimize the risk:

- *Loan approval.* Buyer-financing problems are the number one reason houses don't close and are behind half of all failed escrows, said Bill. The five offers we got all came with a letter from each buyer's direct lender saying that the buyer had been preapproved for the loan. That's pretty standard. To make sure, get bank statements, credit reports, and income verification up front.
- *Appraisal.* Getting a home to be appraised for the purchase price is often a big problem. Banks base loans on either the purchase price or the appraised value, whichever is lower. Thus, if a buyer is taking out an 80 percent loan, the bank will lend 80 percent of the lower number.

    To appraise a house, a licensed appraiser looks at the most recent sales of similar properties in the area to find what are called comps, or comparable properties. The appraiser then looks at the subject property and evaluates it for condition, upgrades, size of both home and lot, and level of finishes to determine its market value. This exercise, though partly subjective, is supposed to protect both buyers and lenders. If the house appraisal comes in lower than the selling price, the buyer has to pay more or the seller has to lower the price or the deal is dead.

Low appraisals kill about 40 percent of escrows, said Bill, who talked to our buyer's lender, who contacted his appraiser to find out whether the house would appraise in the ballpark. Then Bill had the buyer agree that if the house appraised for up to $10,000 less than the purchase price, the buyer would pay the difference. The home appraised at the purchase price.

- *Home inspection.* Buyers should have an inspection done within a week of opening escrow. Deals rarely fall apart over a home's physical condition, but buyers can use these reports to get sellers to lower the price, make repairs, or both. All the more reason to have the house in good repair before you list it.

- *Title clearance.* A property's title lists who owns it and any liens against it, which owners are often unaware of. A house has to be clear of liens to transfer to a new owner, and all the owners must agree to sell. Title issues rarely end deals but can hold them up. Look at your home's title for problems before you list the house.

- *Contingencies.* Many buyers make offers that are contingent on another transaction, such as their house closing escrow. "If you have a buyer in escrow on his house, take a hard look at how solid that deal is," Bill said.

The End of an Era

Bill took the sale documents to Dad's hospital bed, where Dad signed them and green-lighted the property's handoff to a new family. When the escrow closed on April 9, Dad sighed as much as his lungs would let him. His job was done. Between that, his pension, and his life insurance policies, his bride of sixty-two years would be well taken care of. Knowing that, he could breathe a little easier. Fifteen days later, Dad died as he lived, elegantly and on his own terms.

Here I am (back left) with my mother, Nancy Jameson, father, Neal Jameson, and older brother, Craig Jameson, in the lobby of the assisted living center in Stanton, California, where my parents moved in May 2012.

The Last Word: Some Housekeeping

Over these last few years, as I have written and read and ruminated about the meaning of stuff, I have come to realize why we—you and I—don't like to get rid of our belongings. It's because consciously or unconsciously, we think they define us. By extension, we don't like to get rid of our loved ones' belongings because we believe they define them, that they embody them somehow, as if with an umbilical connection.

The more we believe that, the harder it is to let go.

After what I have gone through, my value system *and* my psyche have both undergone a remodel. I now see what is blatantly obvious but hard to concede. Are you ready?

We are not our stuff. Our loved ones are not their stuff.

You know that, you say. However, we all—and let's be honest or what are we doing here?—believe to some extent that stuff defines us and those we love.

The more we have, the more we are, or so we think. The

more we have of theirs, the more we have of them. We get caught up in getting our identity from (fill in the blank) our house, car, clothes, art collection, books, jewelry, letters, awards, collections—and we fear we would cease to exist if it all disappeared.

But those are just trappings.

We are who we are without all that. If we've lived well and loved well, we won't be forgotten. Yet a fear of forgetting or being forgotten makes us cling to stuff like a life preserver that we think we need to keep memories afloat. But the truth is we can swim better without it.

This fear and need to cling to a false sense of security are why millions of adult children have gone through what I went through. And many more will. But it doesn't have to be that way.

If more people lived like the Browns and the Switzes, right-sizing as they went, and fewer lived like Peter Brenton's parents and mine, accumulating and clinging to the bittersweet end, the task of downsizing or clearing the old homestead might actually be, dare I say, a rich, joyous journey made up of reflections and discoveries of a life well lived . . . and well maintained.

A lifetime habit of judicious editing is a gift you give yourself and your children. Living well no matter what your stage in life means letting go as you grow, shedding your old self to make room for the person you're becoming.

THE WEEK OF DAD'S FUNERAL, I got a sympathy card from a friend. (Now condolences were in order.) My friend, who also had recently lost a father she had been very close to, wrote, "Remember, it is a blessing to have loved so deeply."

That sentiment helped me and in fact changed my perspective. Yes, my heart ached. But the only way I could have avoided the depth of my grief was to have loved less.

And you know what? I would not make that trade. Not for a guaranteed lifetime of smooth sailing and even-keeled emotions would I give up loving deeply so that I could avoid grief.

In fact, once I saw mourning as the result of loving, I came to see my grief as a gift.

Heartbreak meant I was fortunate.

When we ache with loss, we realize not only that we have cared but also what matters. And it's not the stuff. I do not miss Dad's things. I miss Dad. I do have photos of him that I like to look at and that bring him back in a sense. I have some letters he wrote me and a wooden Patties cigar box that sits on my desk and holds pens and pencils. The wooden box came from a factory where Dad worked as a boy shortly after the Depression. He made cigars alongside my grandfather.

It reminds me where he came from and where I came from, but mostly it reminds me to be grateful of all I have and have had, including parents who taught me what matters.

So, MY FRIENDS, KEEP WHAT YOU LOVE and what nurtures you. Hold dear your memories along with a few treasures from those who loved you and whom you loved. Leave a few treasures for those you love to remember you by. But do so judiciously.

Beyond that, live well, love deeply, and hold on to a heartful—not a houseful—of memories. That will be plenty. I promise.

Acknowledgments

The title of "author" endows me with more billing than I deserve. In truth, this book simply would not be here were it not for an entire scaffolding of support, an infrastructure to which I would like to reserve a special spot in heaven with all-down bedding, and an ambrosia-filled cornucopia.

In my constellation, I am fortunate to have many bright stars:

My agent Linda Konner, who not only quickly recognized the need for this book, but also had the great instinct to broaden its scope by asking me to write it not only for adult children faced with clearing out a parent's home, but also for older adults who don't want to leave a burden to their children.

My editor Barbara Berger, who brought clarity and order to my copy when I felt like I was dancing with an armful of smoke, and the rest of the team at Sterling Publishing, who further tamed and tidied my prose and created a beautiful design to get it between these covers.

At AARP, Book Division Director Jodi Lipson, who agreed with Linda's big-picture thinking, and enthusiastically added AARP's endorsement for this book, expanding our horizons exponentially.

My extraordinary posse of editors in newsrooms across America who run my weekly syndicated home design and lifestyle column, and routinely make me look better than I am.

My honest and loyal readers whose emails not only keep me in line, but teach, inspire, and remind me why I do what I do.

My thousand and one sources who have trusted me to serve as a conduit for their ideas and advice, especially my sounding boards Stephanie Abarbanel, Susan Beane, Mark Brunetz, and Aaron LaPedis.

My loving, wise and wonderful parents, Neal and Nancy Jameson. Mom and Dad, thank you for meeting in Okinawa during World War II, and Dad thank you for pursuing Mom even though she turned your proposal down once, and sent the ring back later. I'm really glad it worked out for you two.

My brother, Craig Jameson, King Solomon incarnate, who has been with me through, well, everything (God bless you and I'm sorry, which I know does not cover it), and his wife, Chiqeeta, who has never met an obstacle she could not completely dismantle with the pure force of her good instincts and charm.

My children, Paige Roth and Marissa Roth, who enrich,

educate, and entertain me endlessly, and who I think even appreciate me, even if they do often say, "When mom is writing a book, dinners get really lousy." Girls, I am doing my level best not to leave you a big mess.

Finally, and not least, my partner Doug Carey, who, besides filling my heart in places I did not even know existed, reviewed this manuscript, offered gentle critiques, and endured and supported me as I wrote and wrestled with it. Thank you for taking this journey with me.

To all of you, please accept my infinite appreciation.

Sources

www.clearingthewayhome.com

www.ebth.com (Everything But The House)

www.griefrecoverymethod.com

www.harvesthelps.org

www.markbrunetz.com

www.maxsold.com

www.millergaffney.com (Miller Gaffney Art Advisory)

www.nasmm.org (National Association of Senior Move Managers®, NASMM) (for survey cited on page 165, see http://www.nasmm.org/press/the_face_of_nasmm.pdf)

www.pauldavislack.com (Davis Laack Stress & Resilience Institute)

www.peterwalshdesign.com

www.theoccasionalwife.com

AARP

AARP print and e-books are available at AARP's online bookstore, www.aarp.org/bookstore, and through local and online bookstores.

Checklist for My Family (AARP.org/ForMyFamily): Guides you through the process of organizing your paperwork: finances, legal documents, online accounts, wishes about medical care, and more.

AARP Livability Index (http://livabilityindex.aarp.org): Plug in your zip codes to help decide where to live or to retire, as it provides the kind of information on schools, housing costs, taxes, weather, local government, community activities, recreation, volunteer opportunities, and a host of other details that factor into decisions about moving to a new locale.

AARP HomeFit Guide (AARP.org/HomeFit): Provides smart solutions for making your home comfortable, safe, and a great fit.

Index